Vintage Botanical Papers

VOLUME 3

End Papers, Junk Journals, Scrapbooking, Origami, Cut-Outs

BASED ON ILLUSTRATIONS BY MAURICE PILLARD VERNEUIL

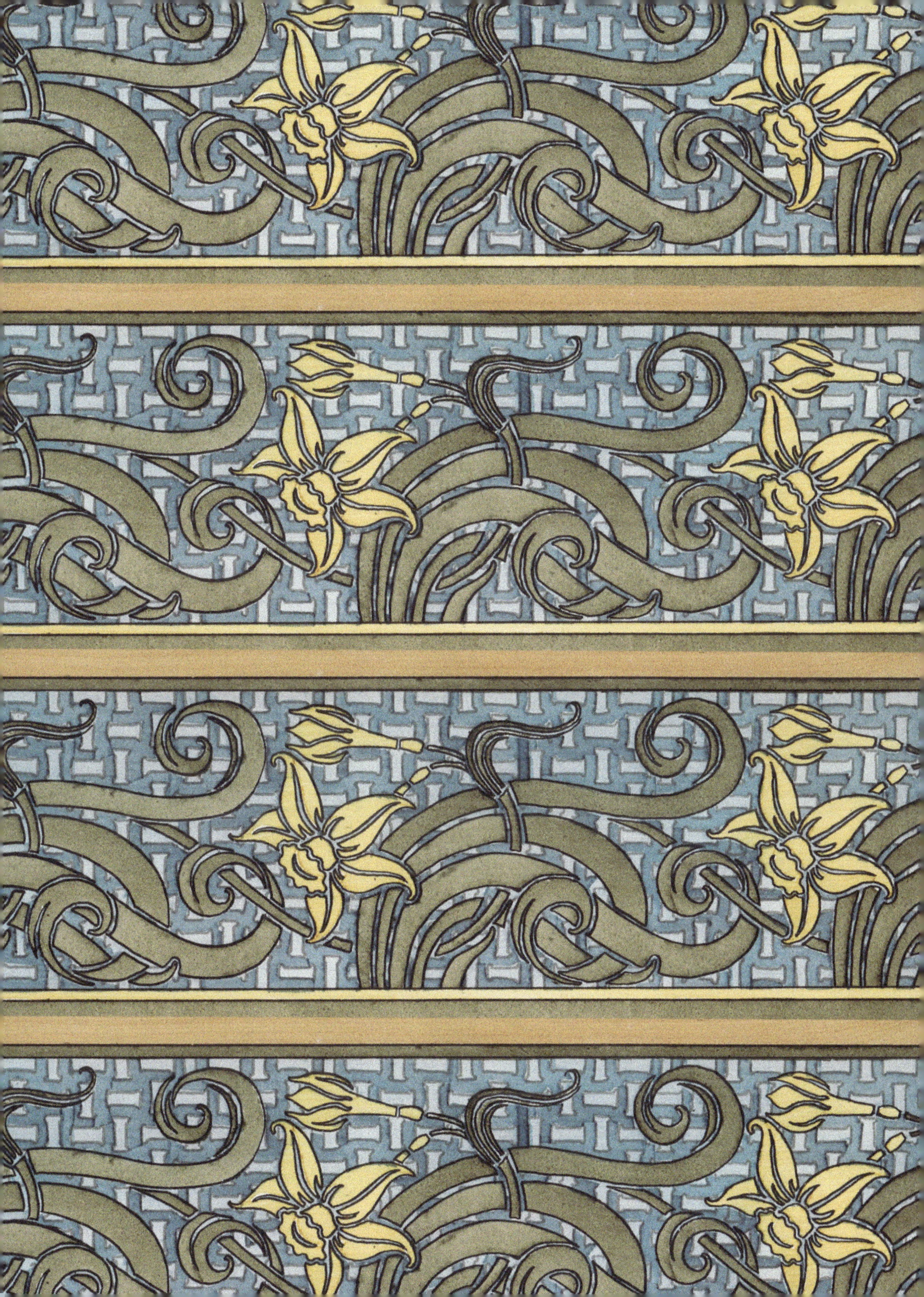

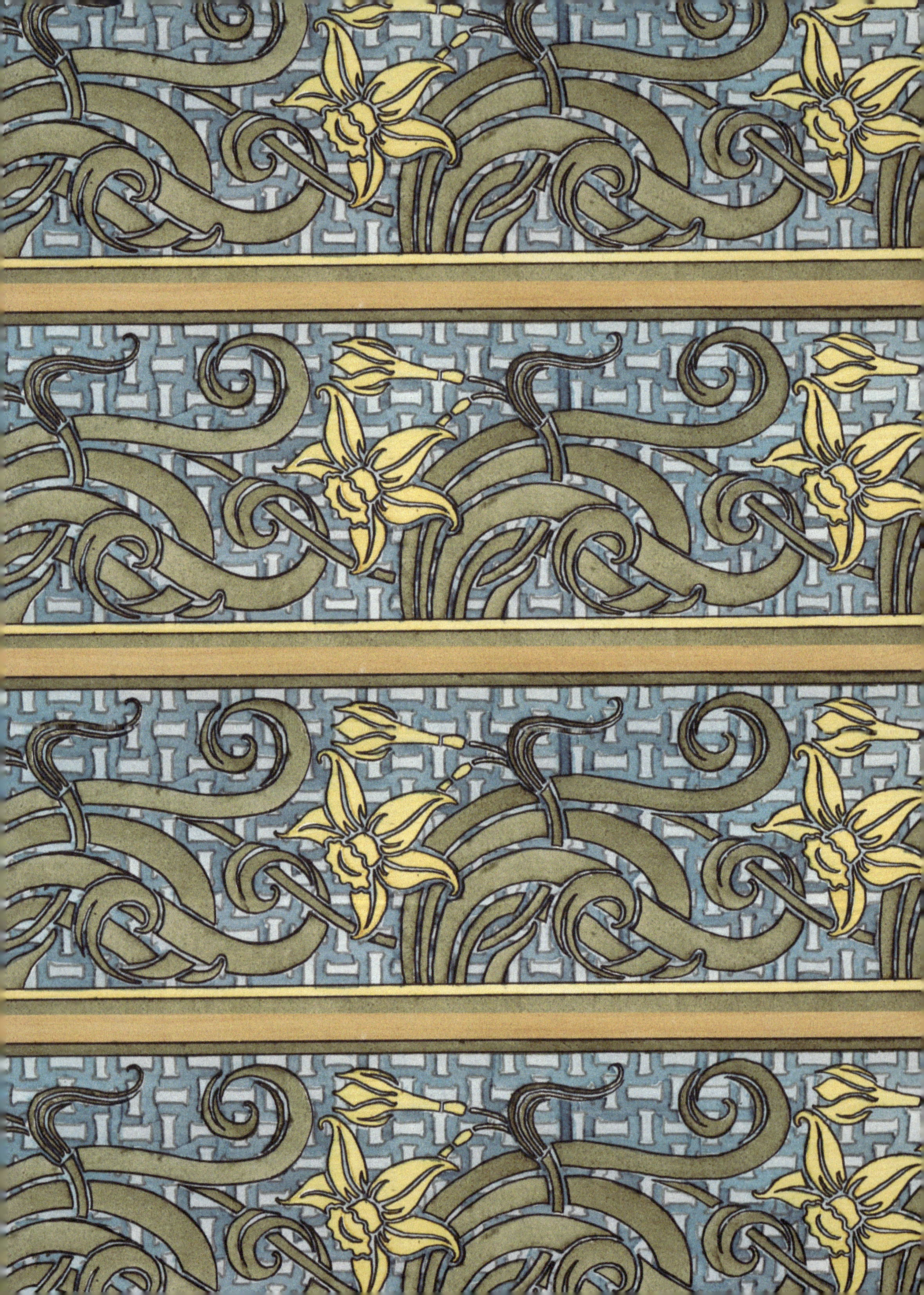

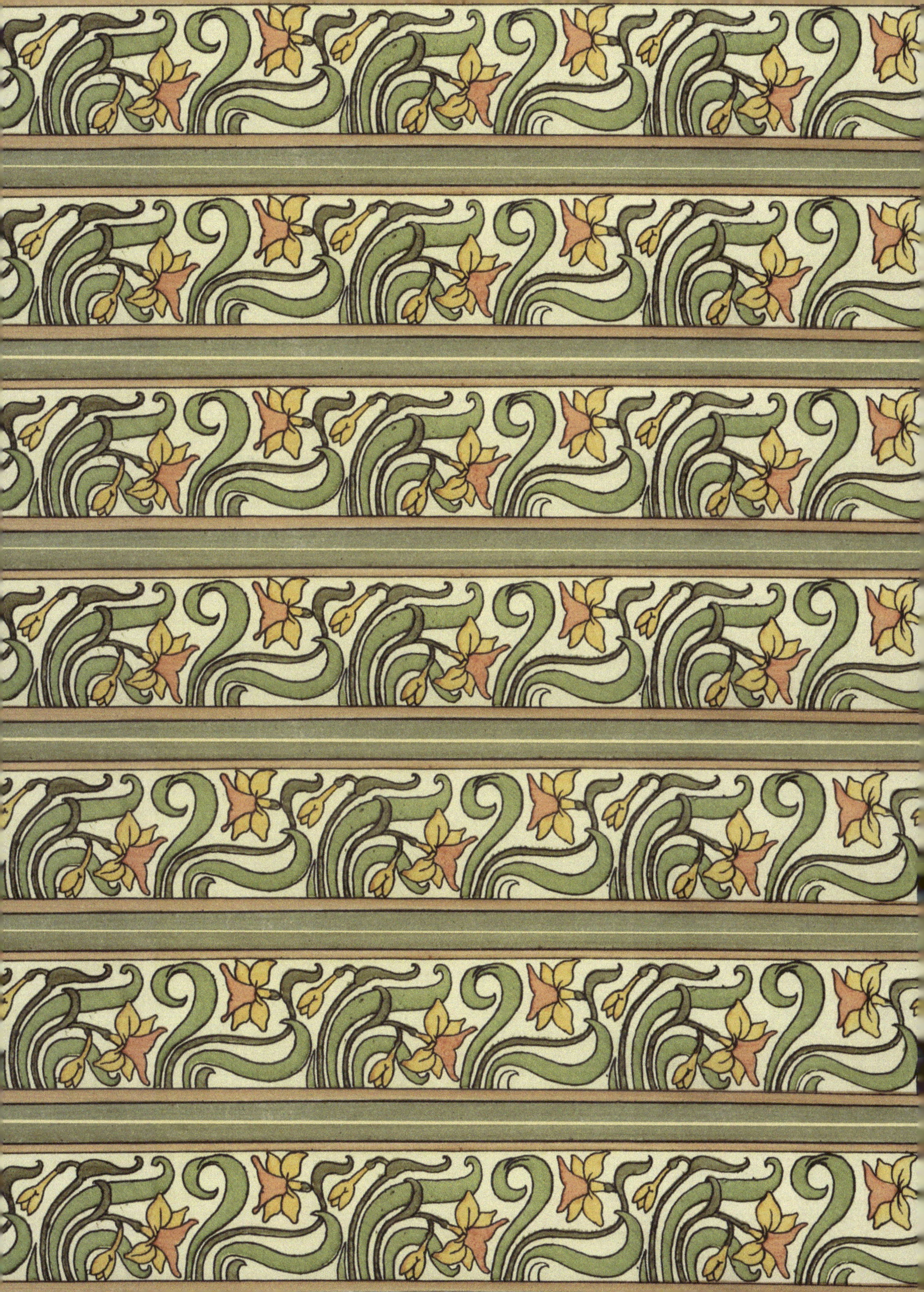

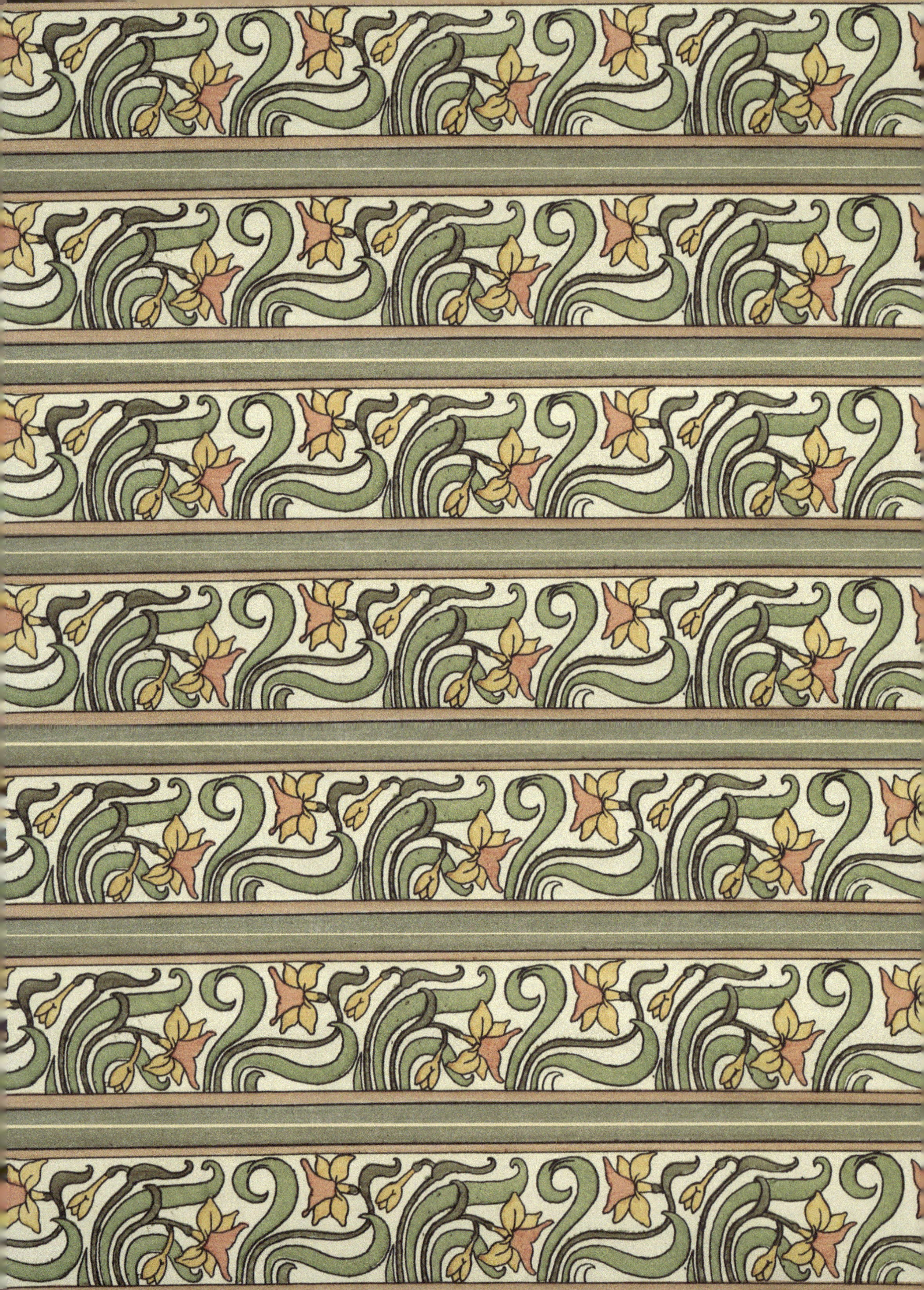

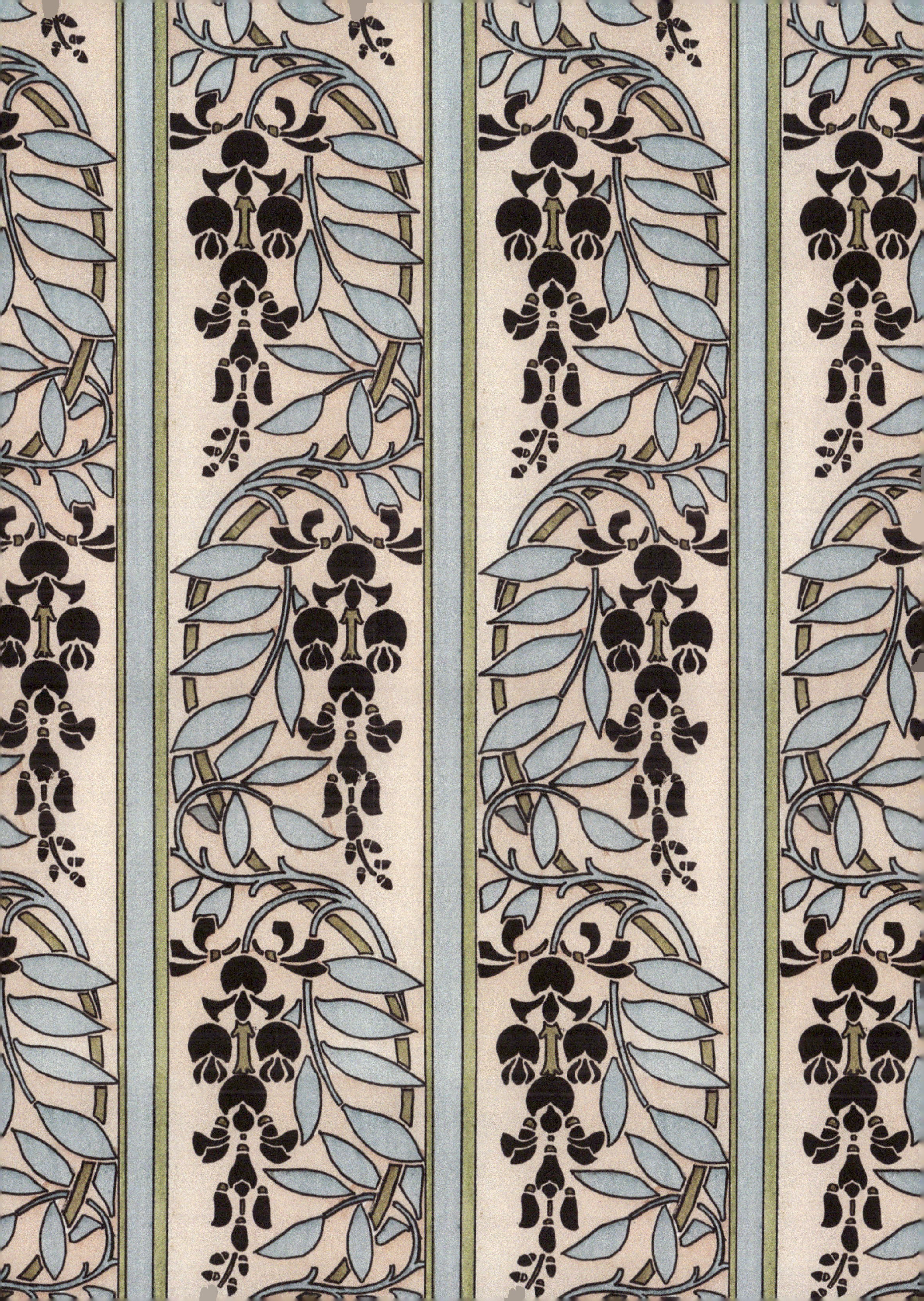

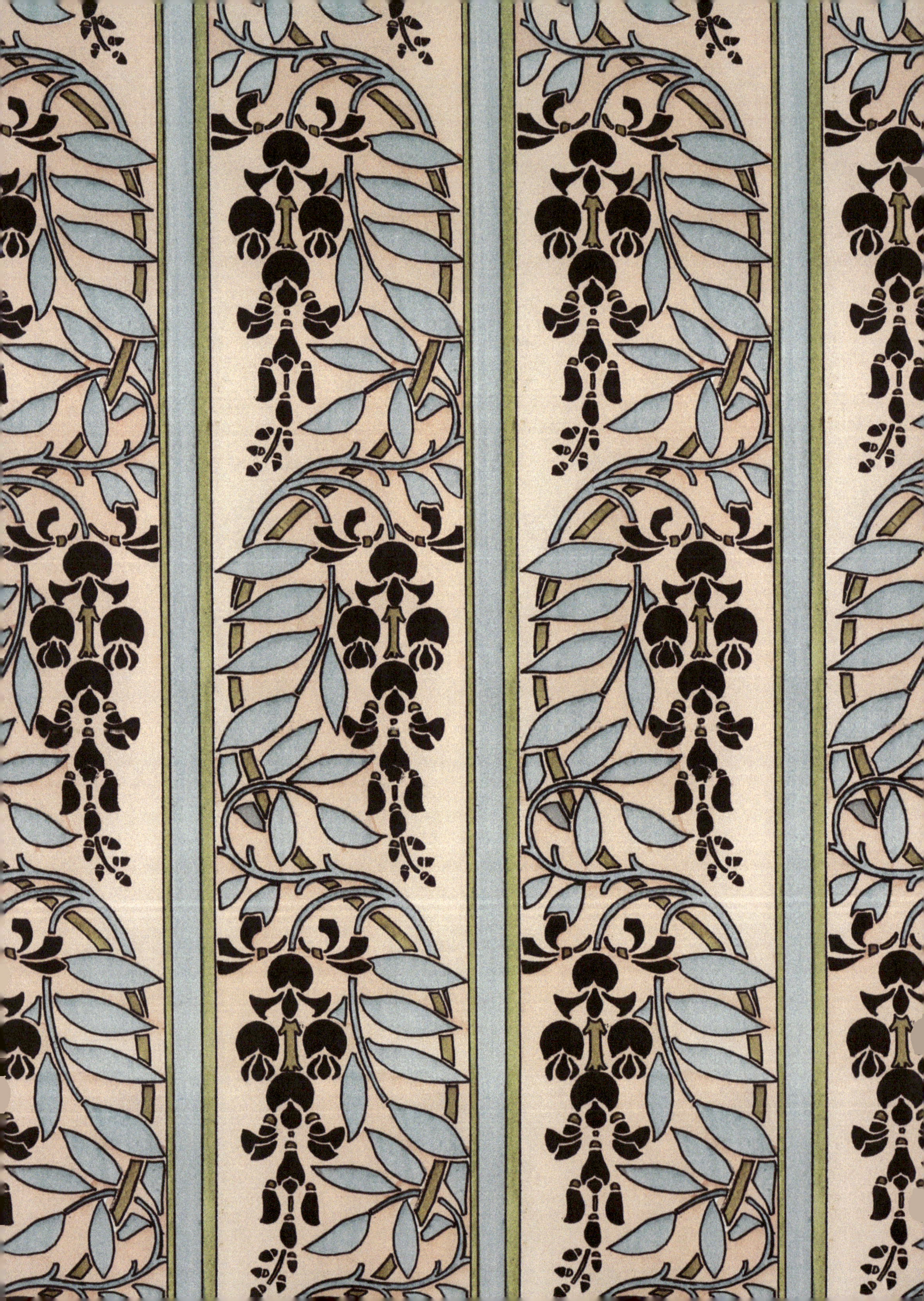

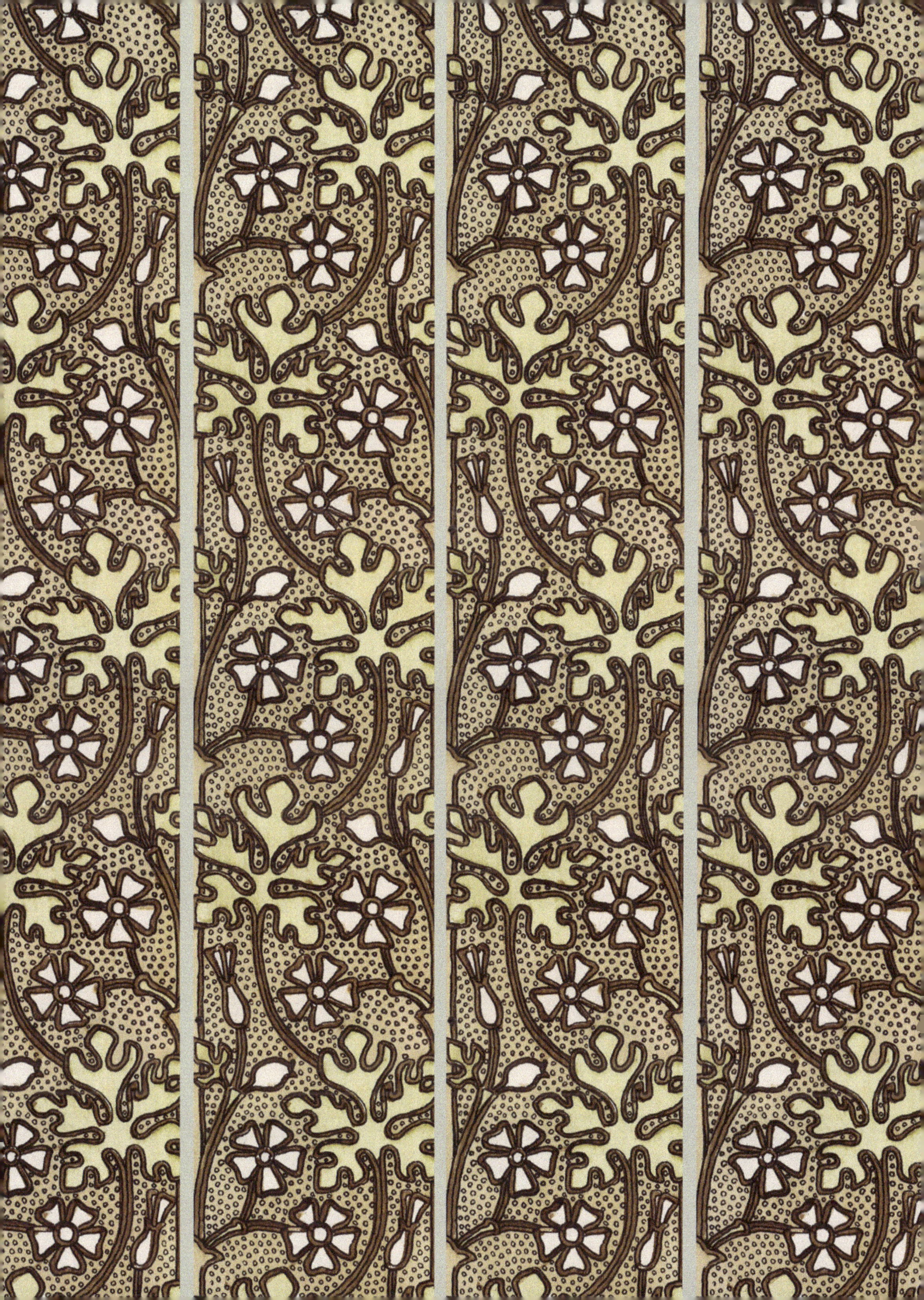

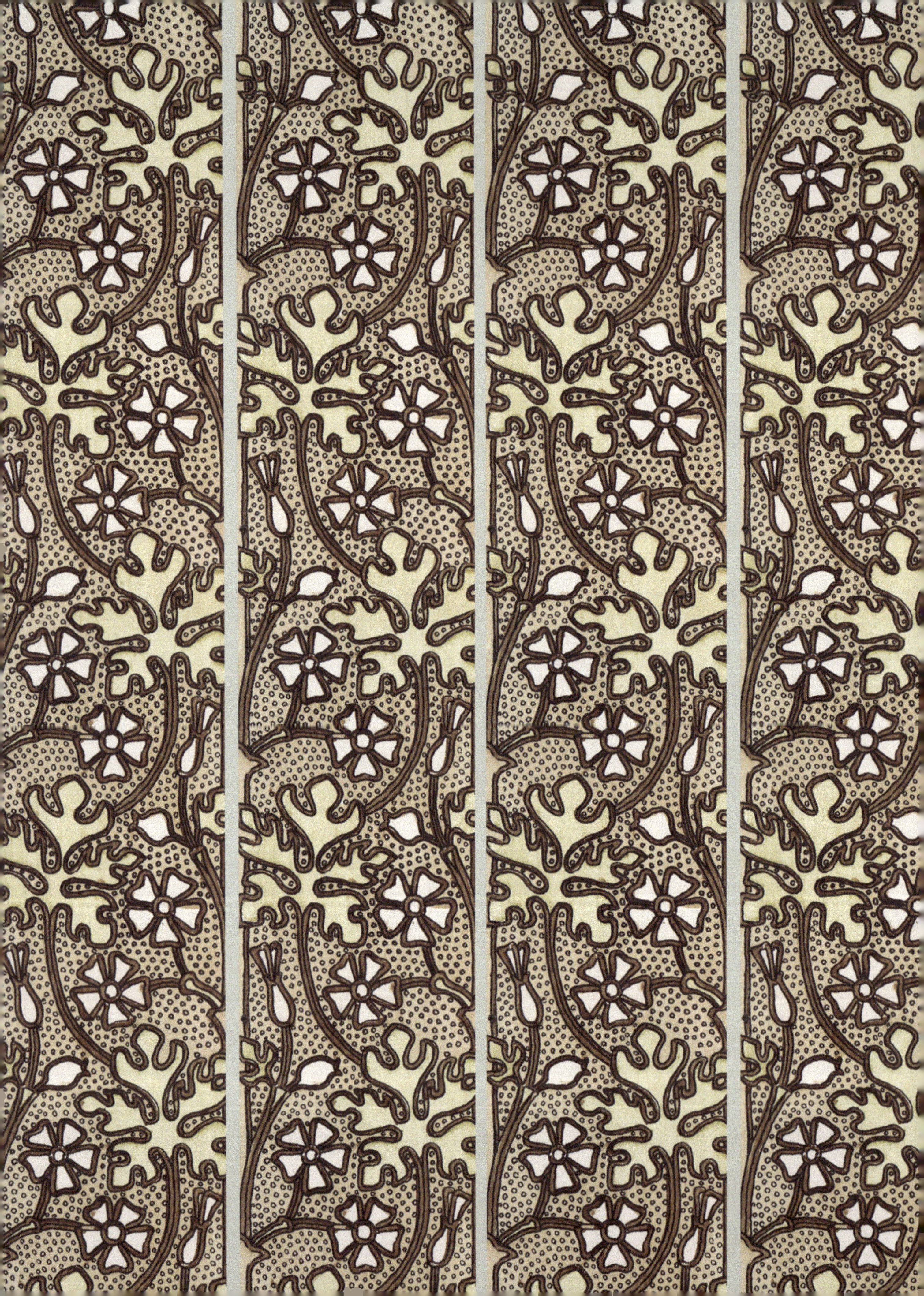

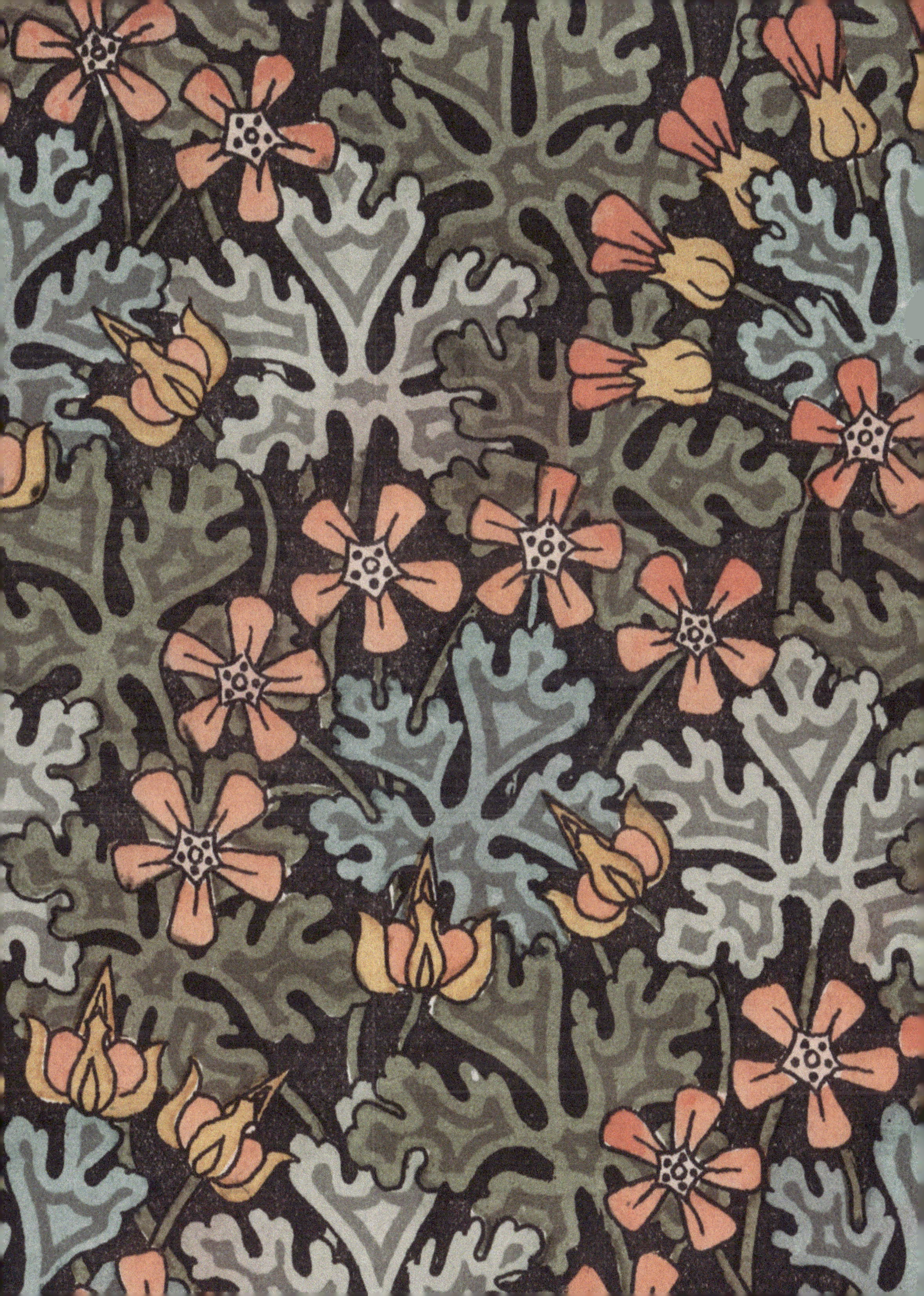

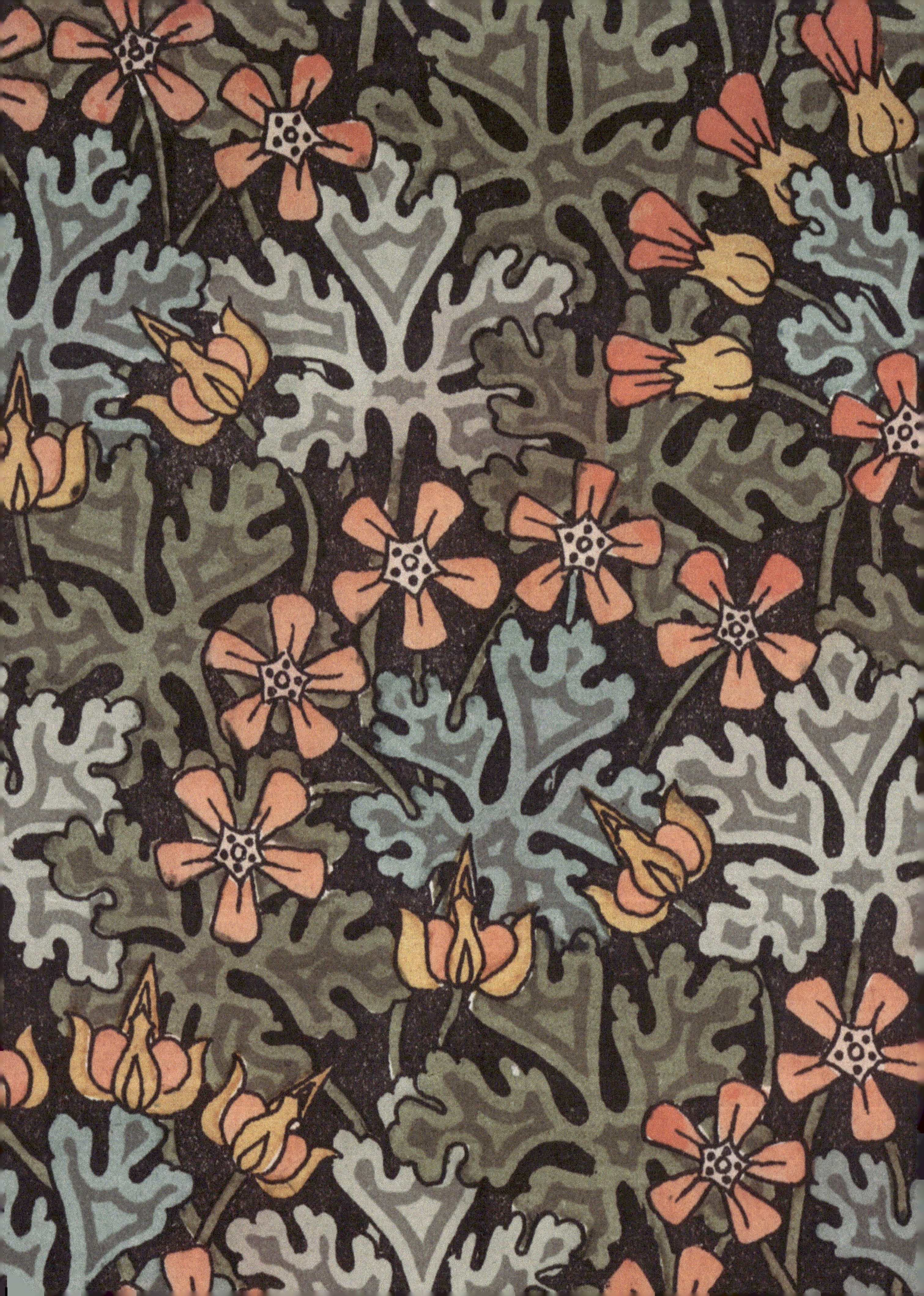

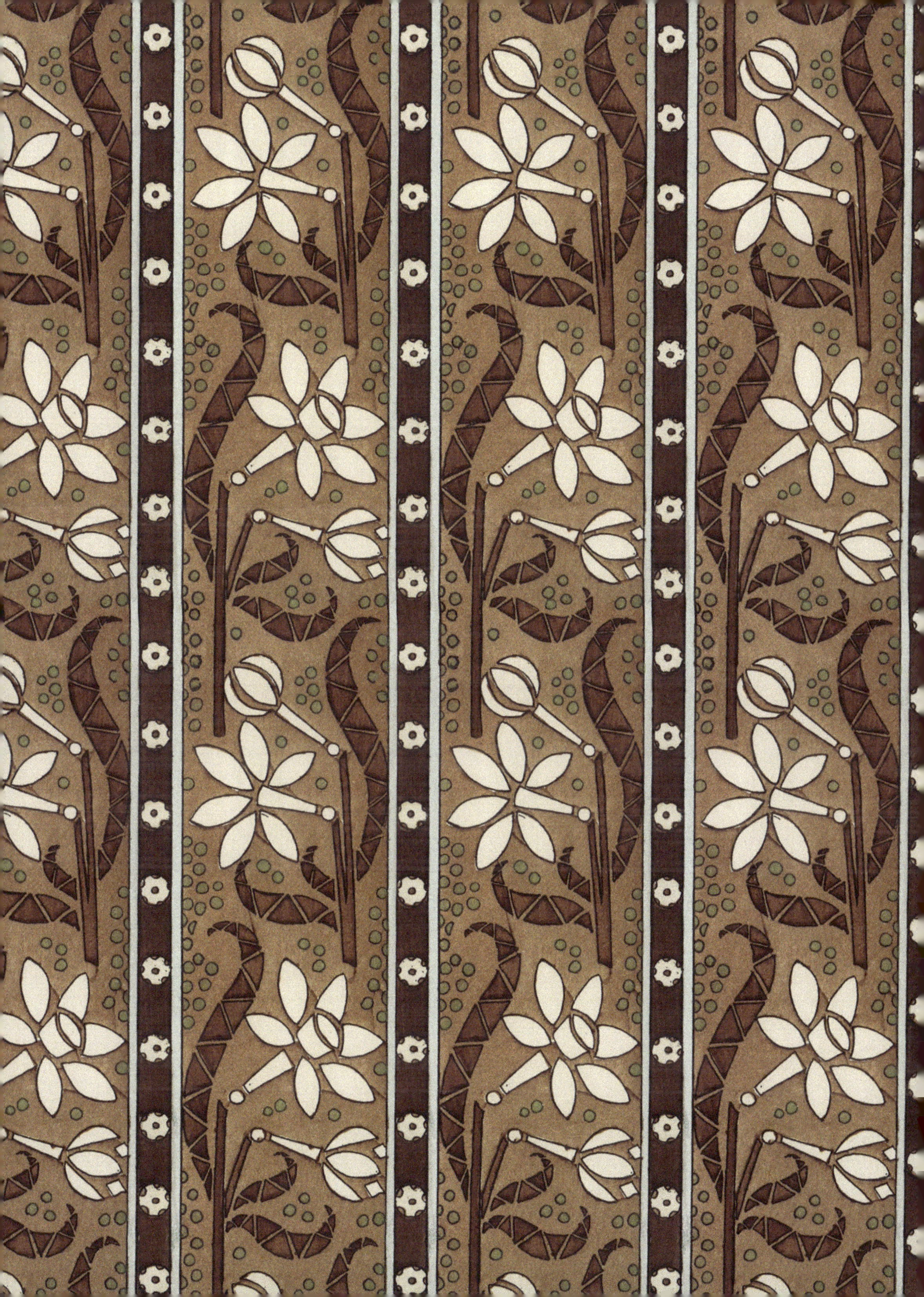

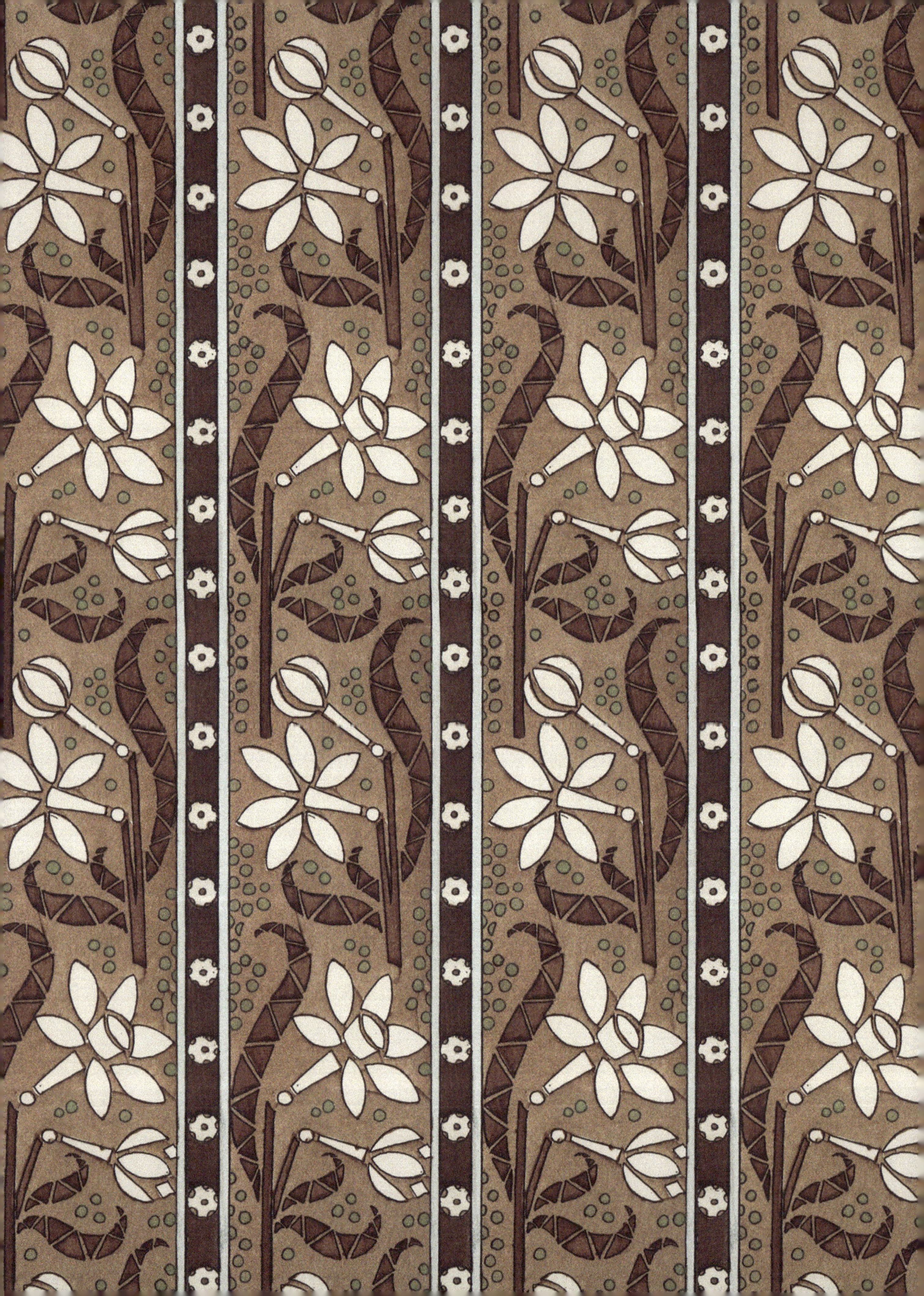

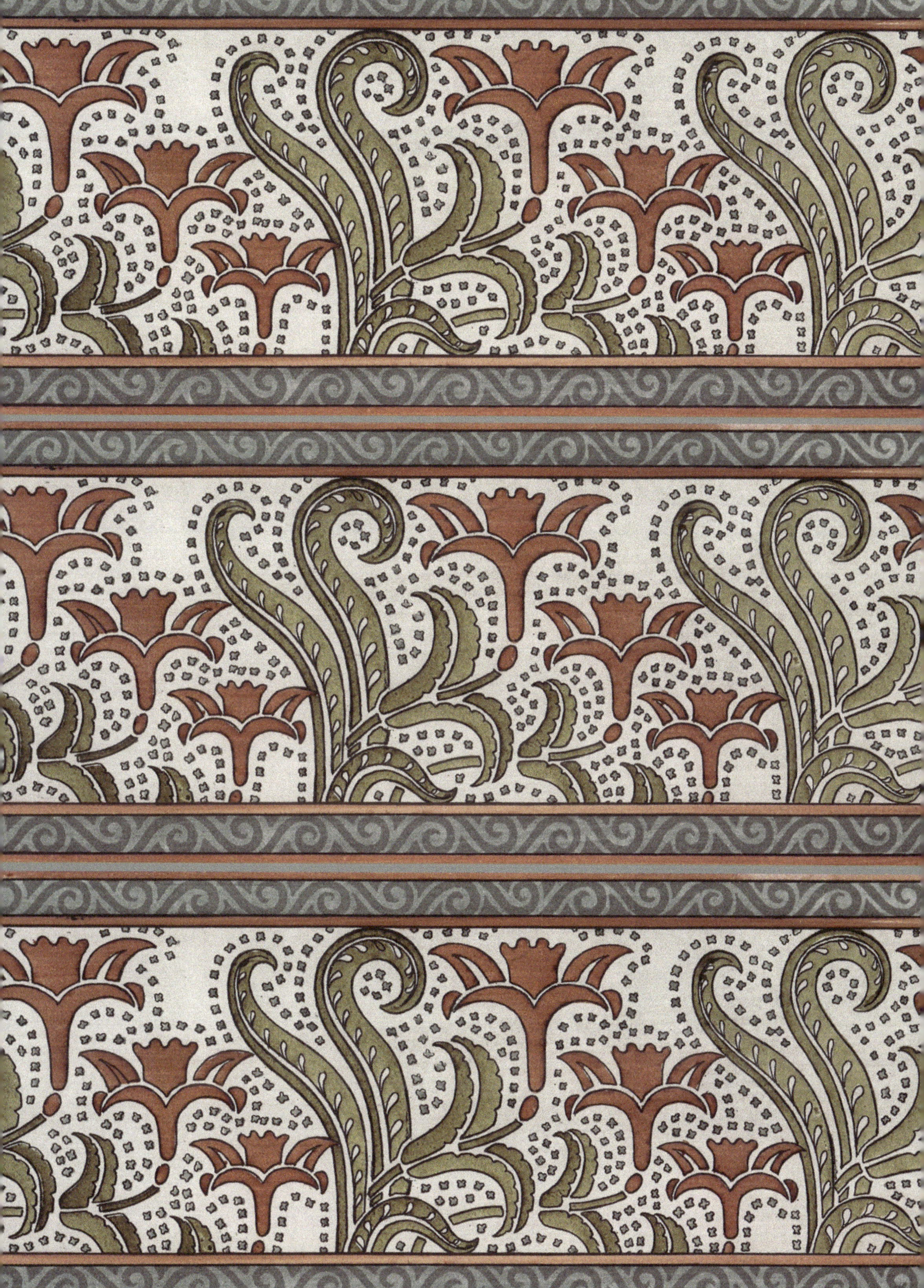

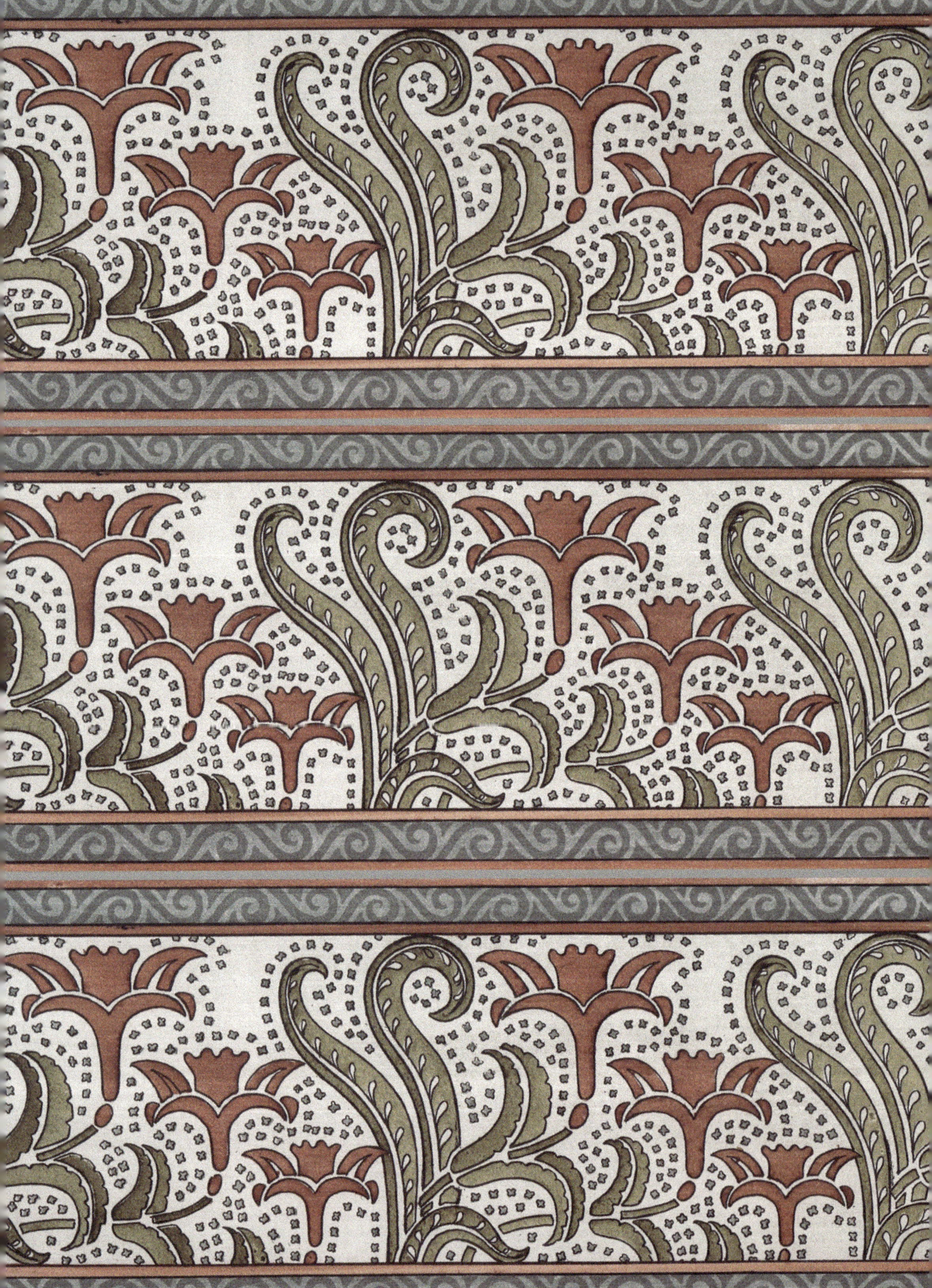

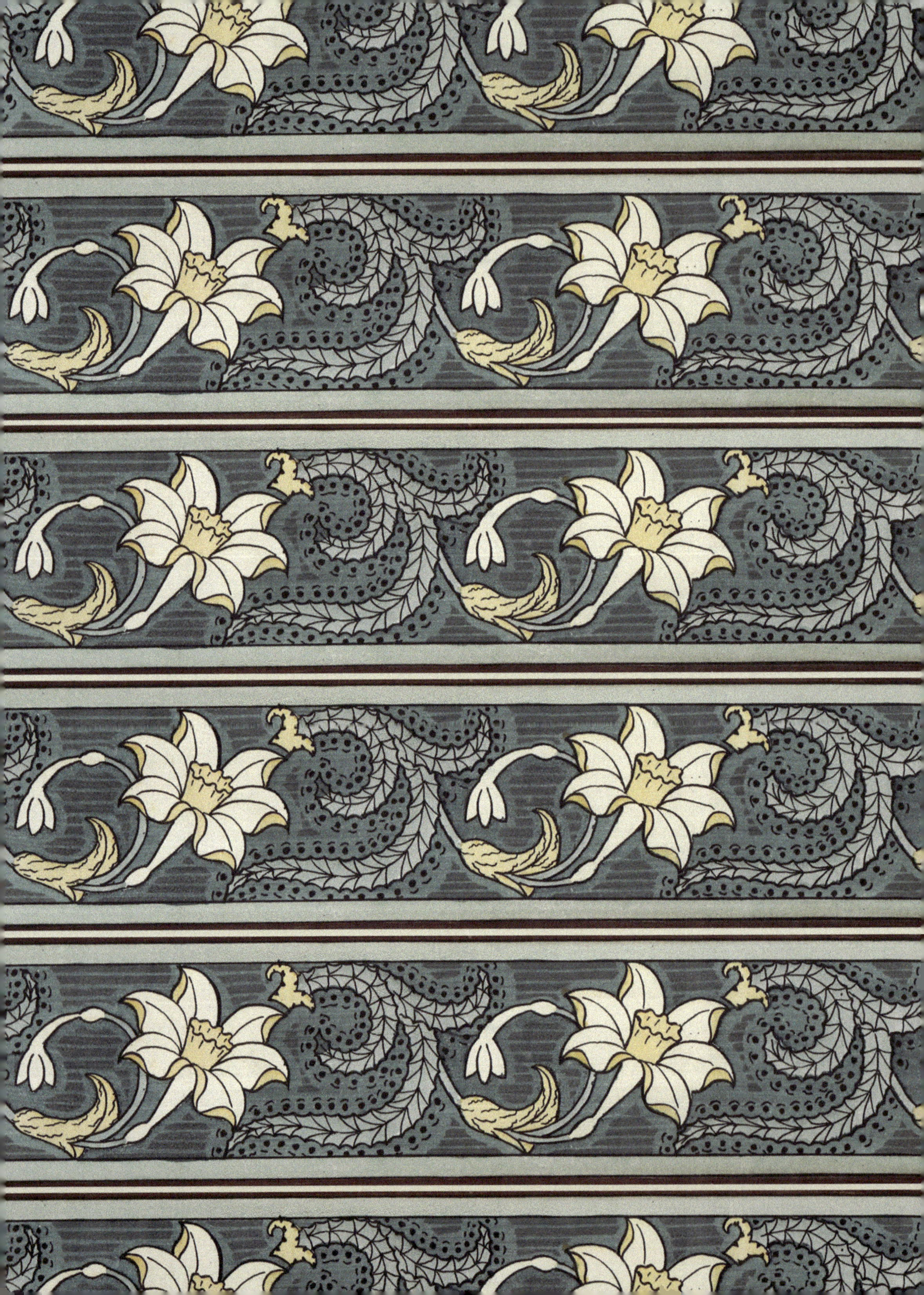

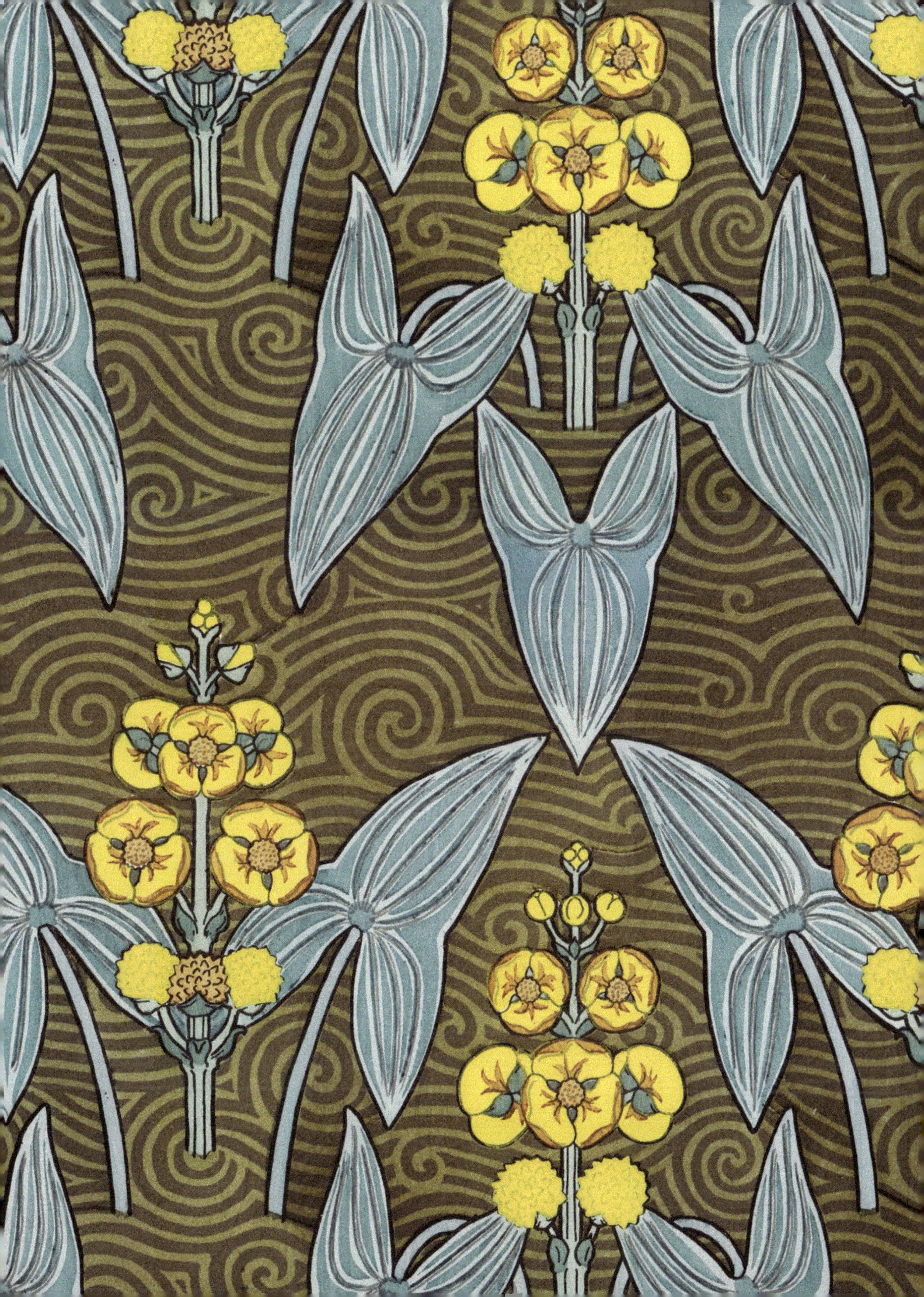

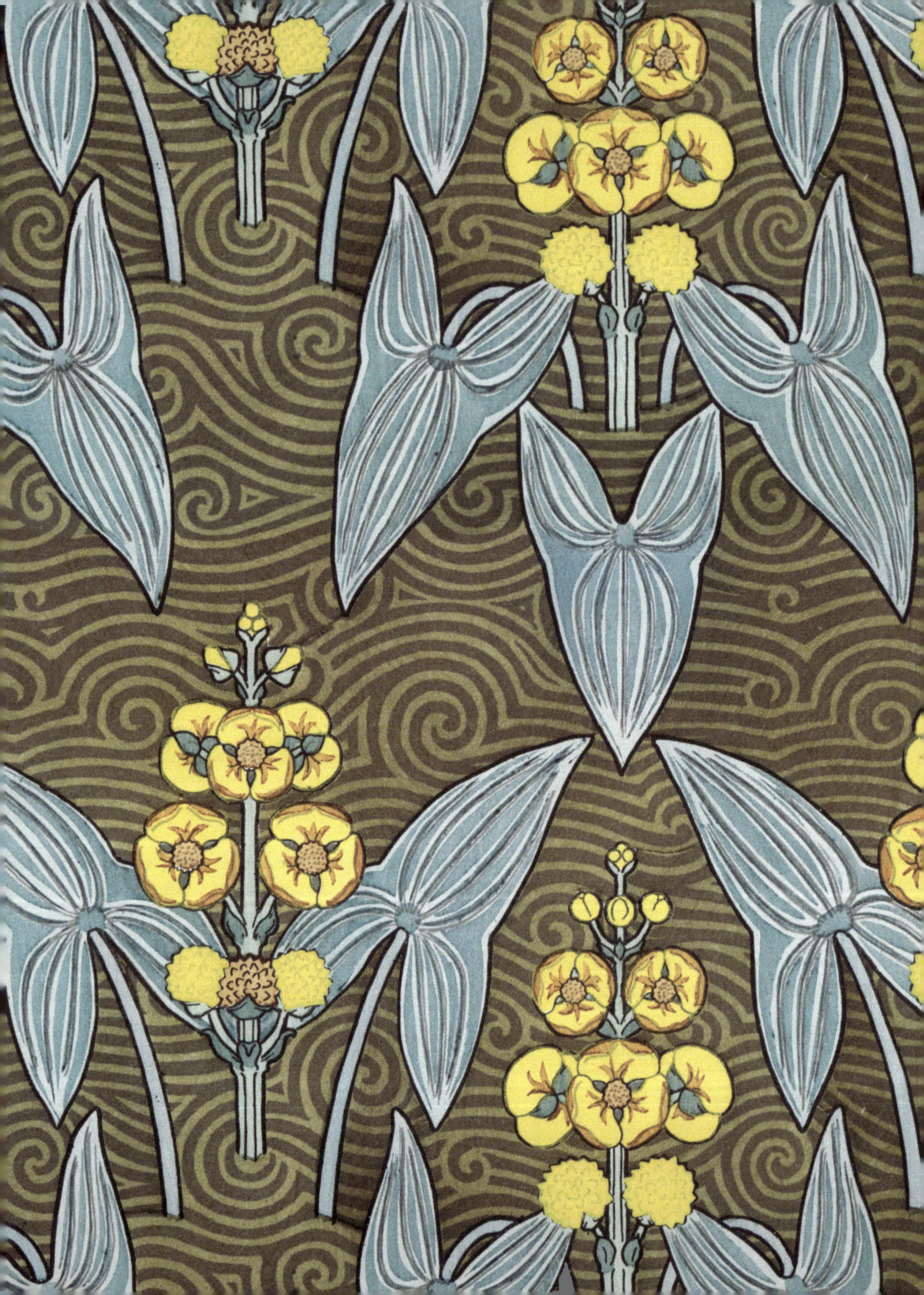

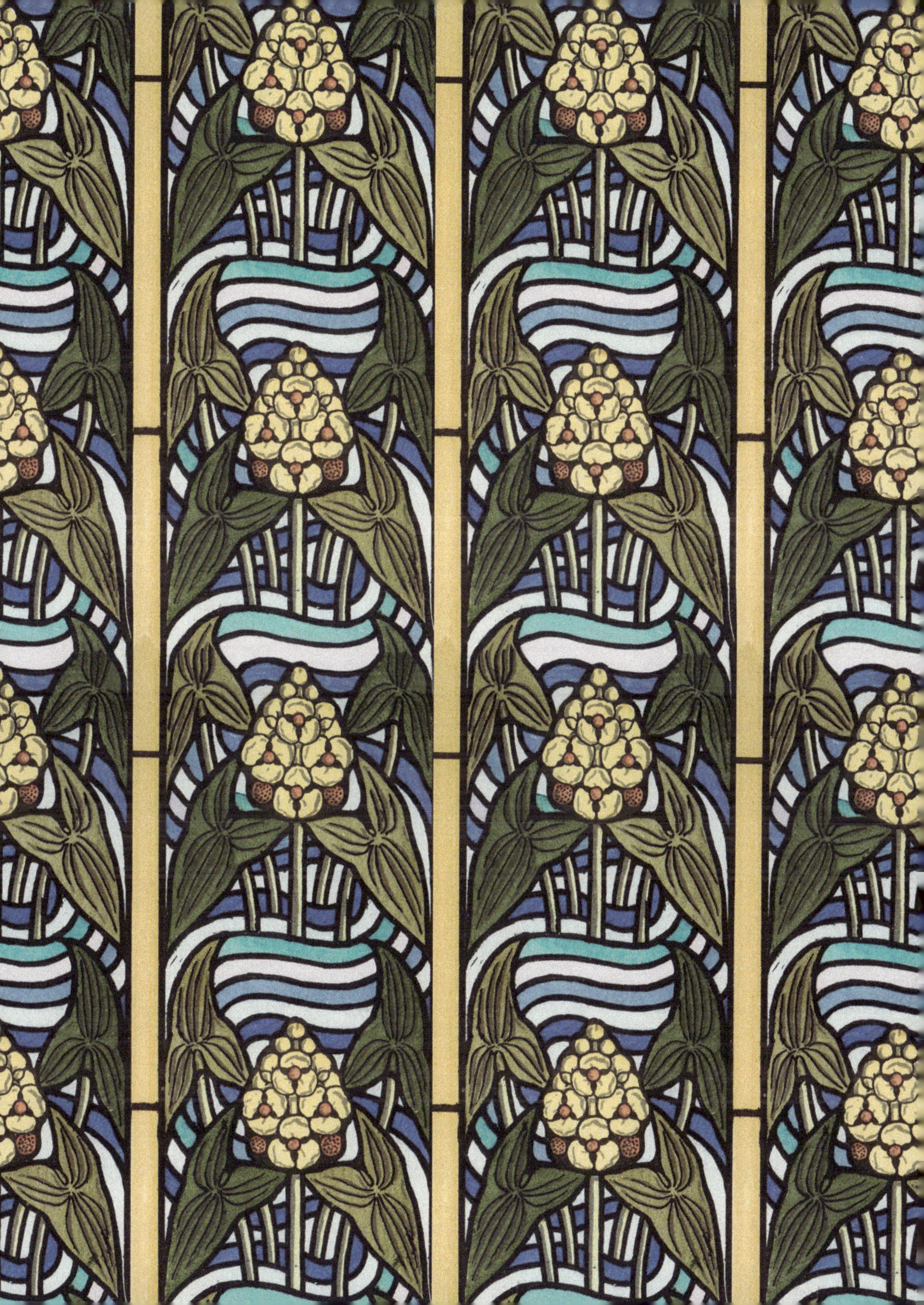

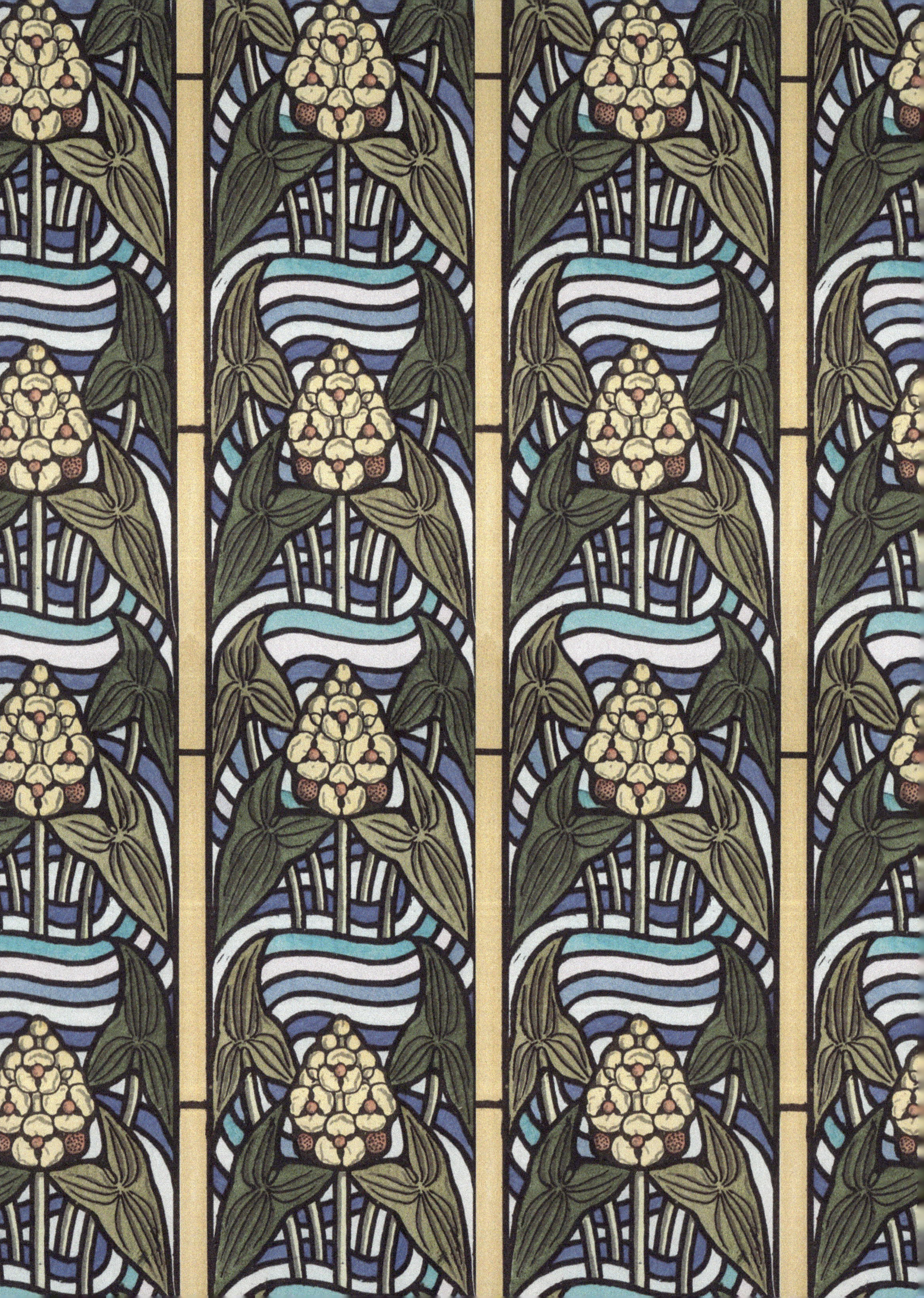

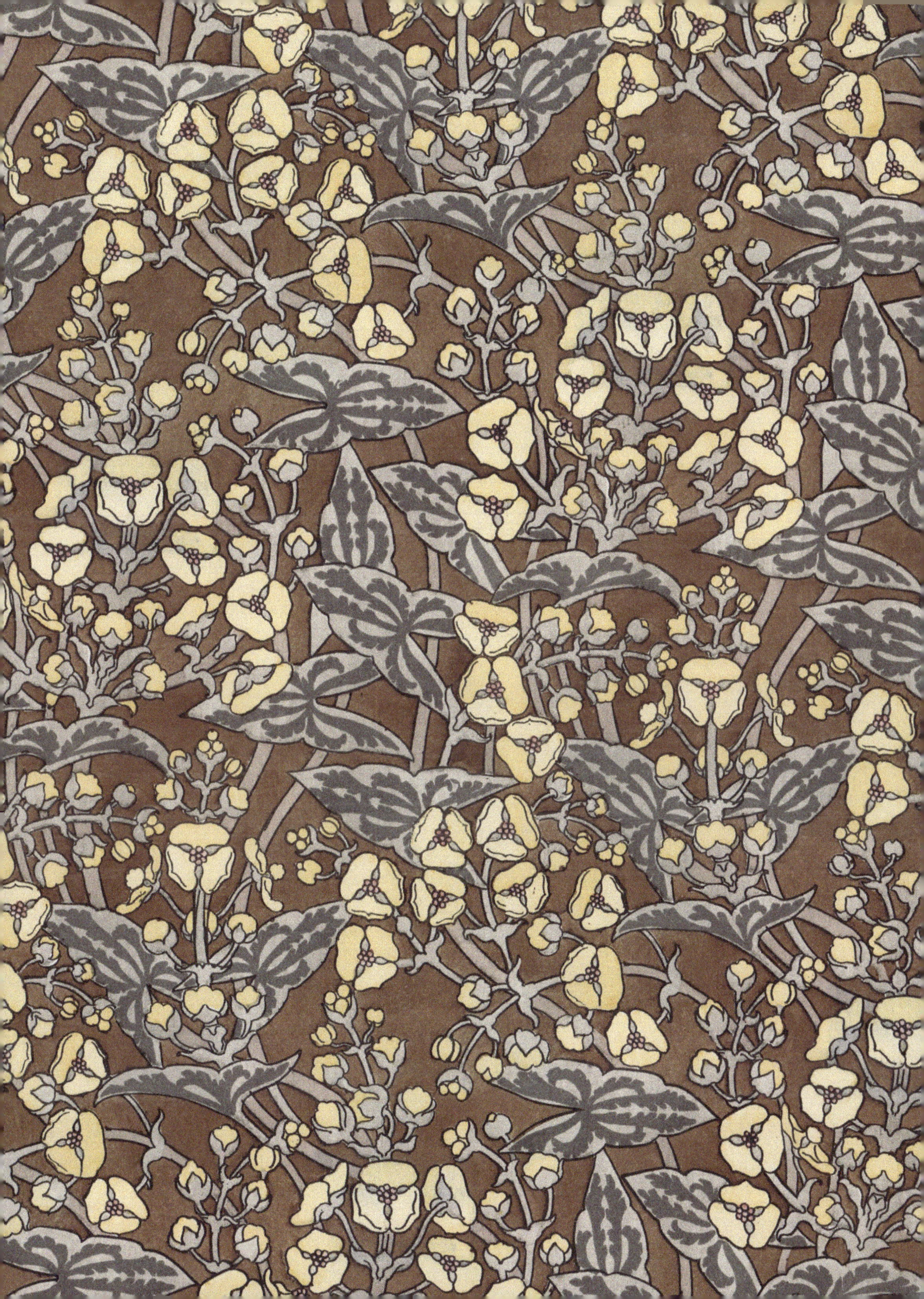

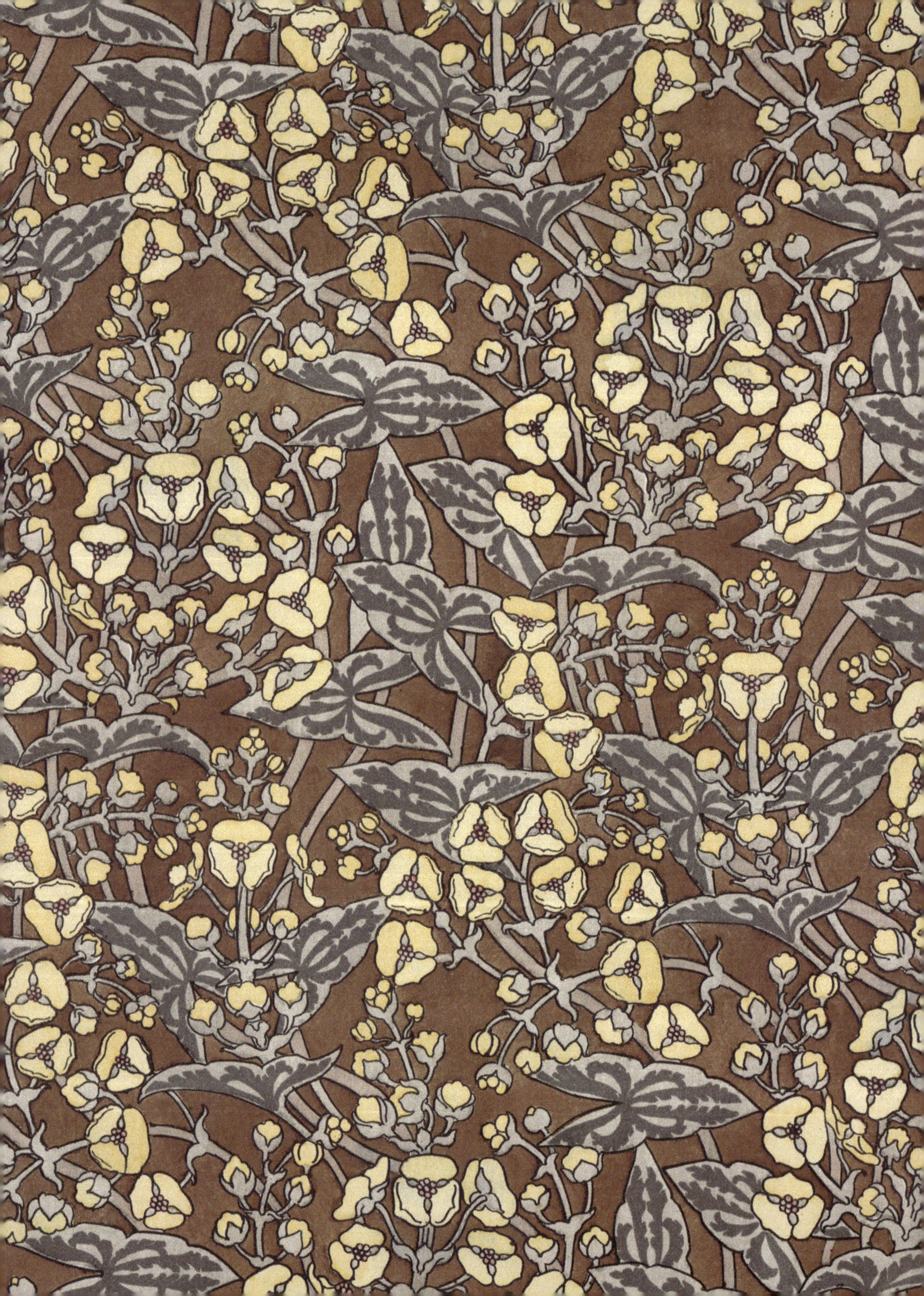

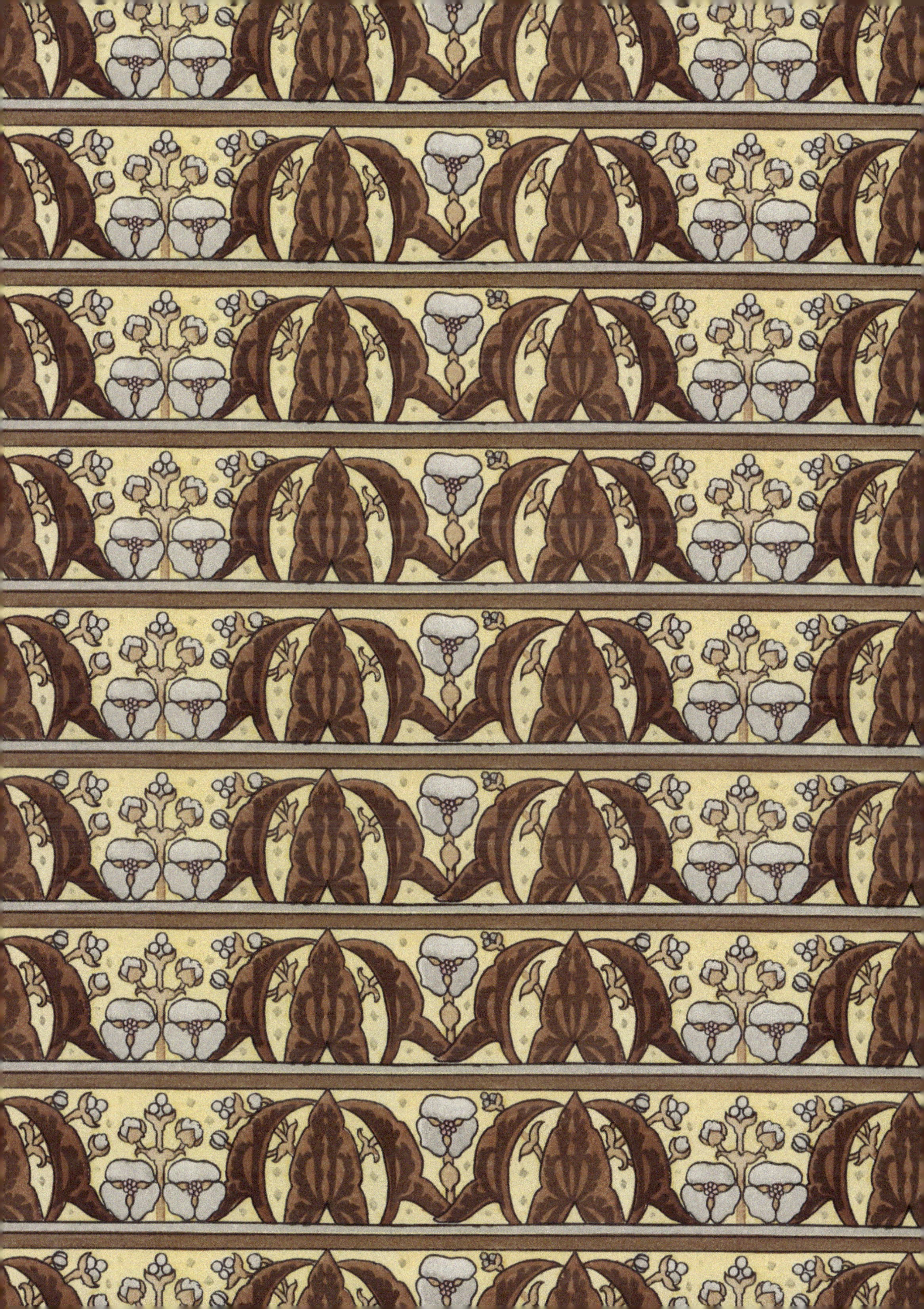

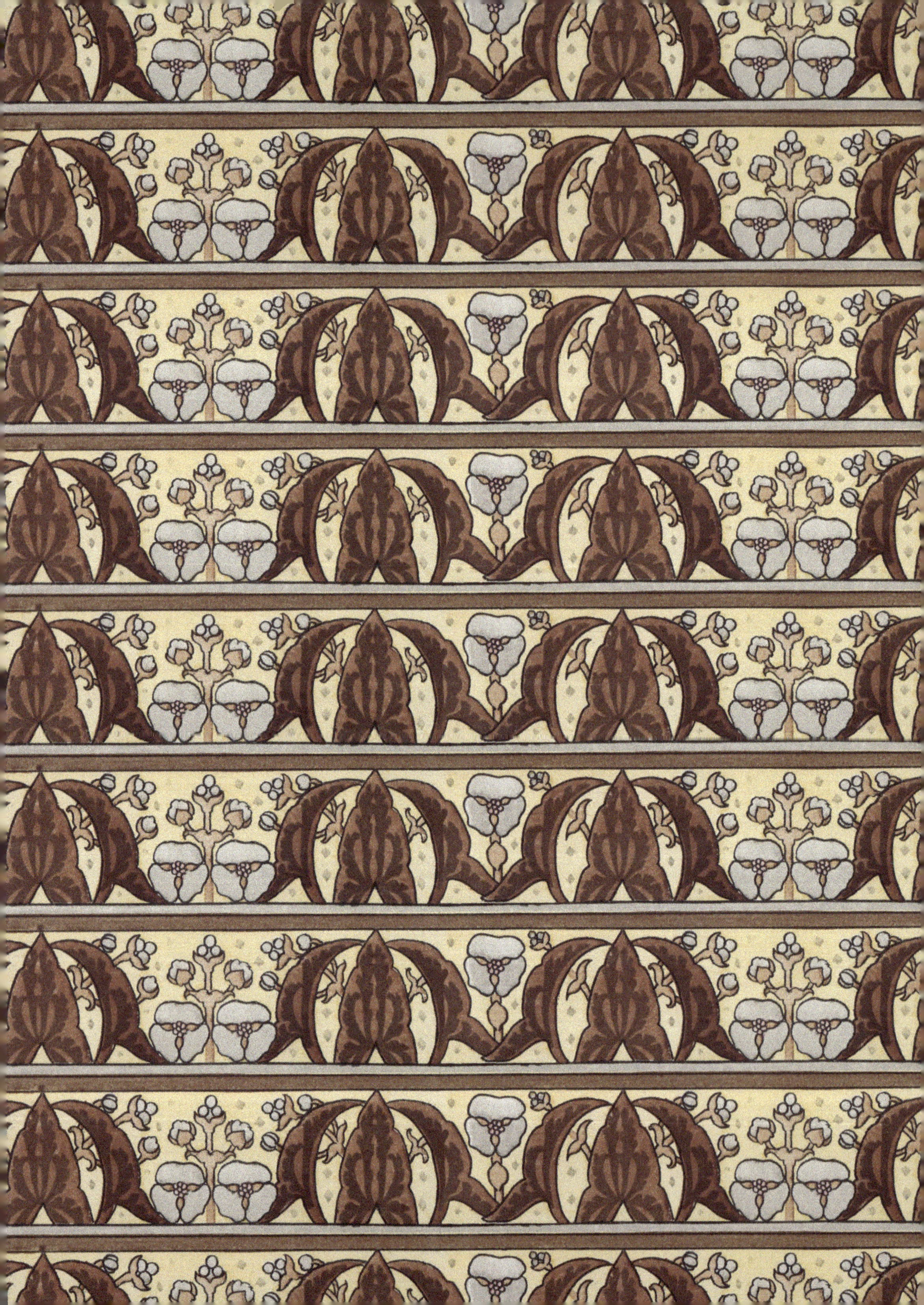

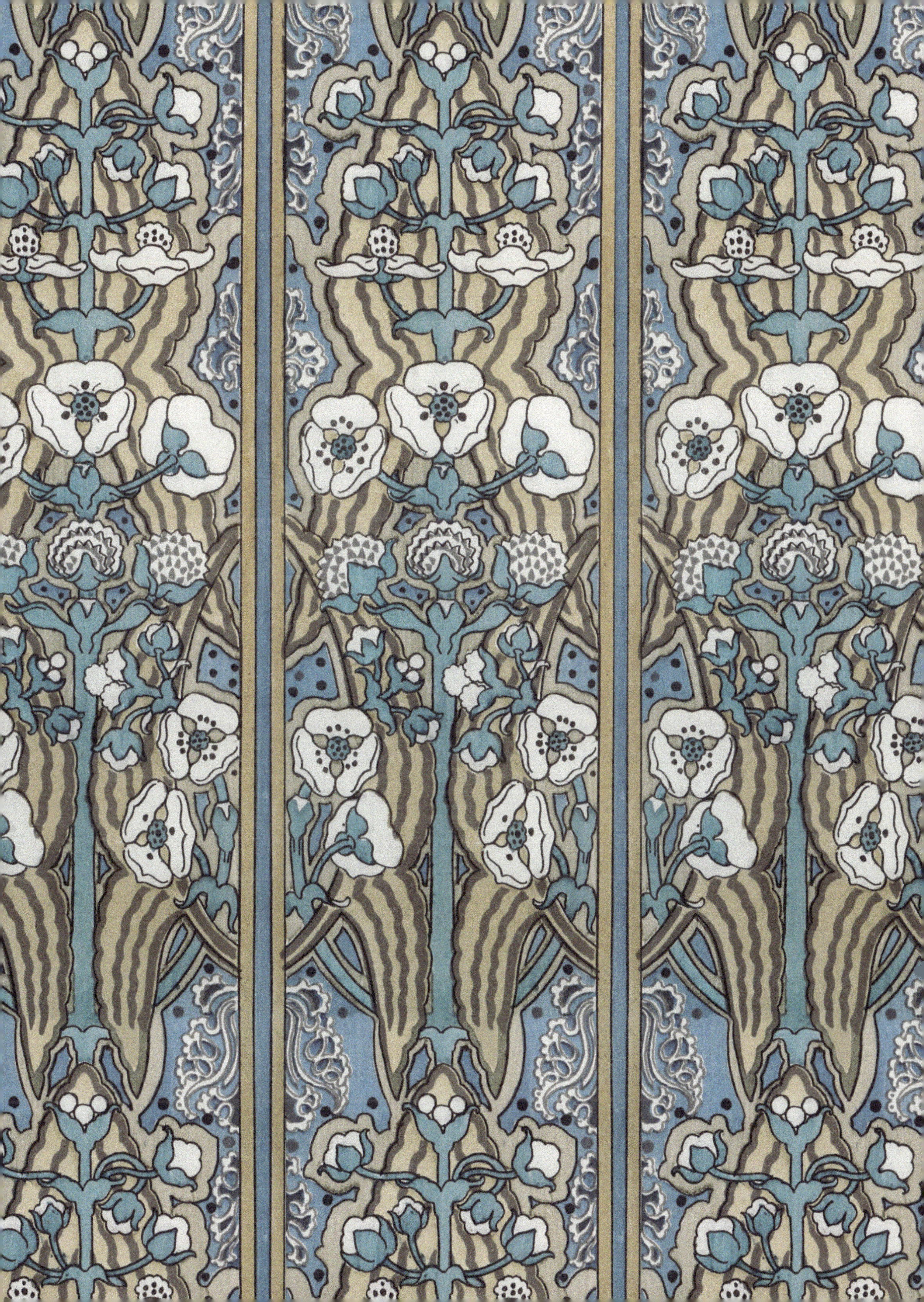

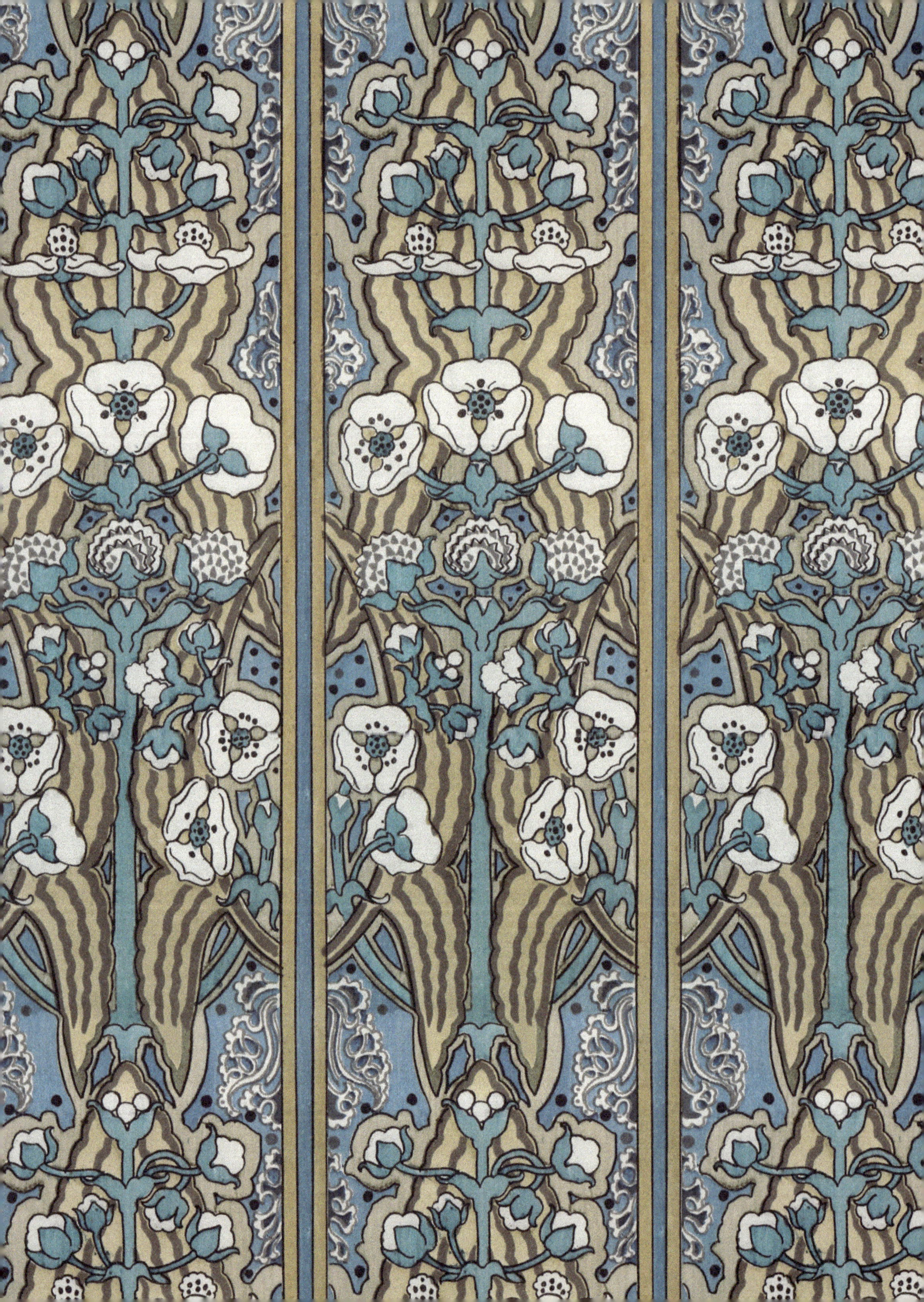

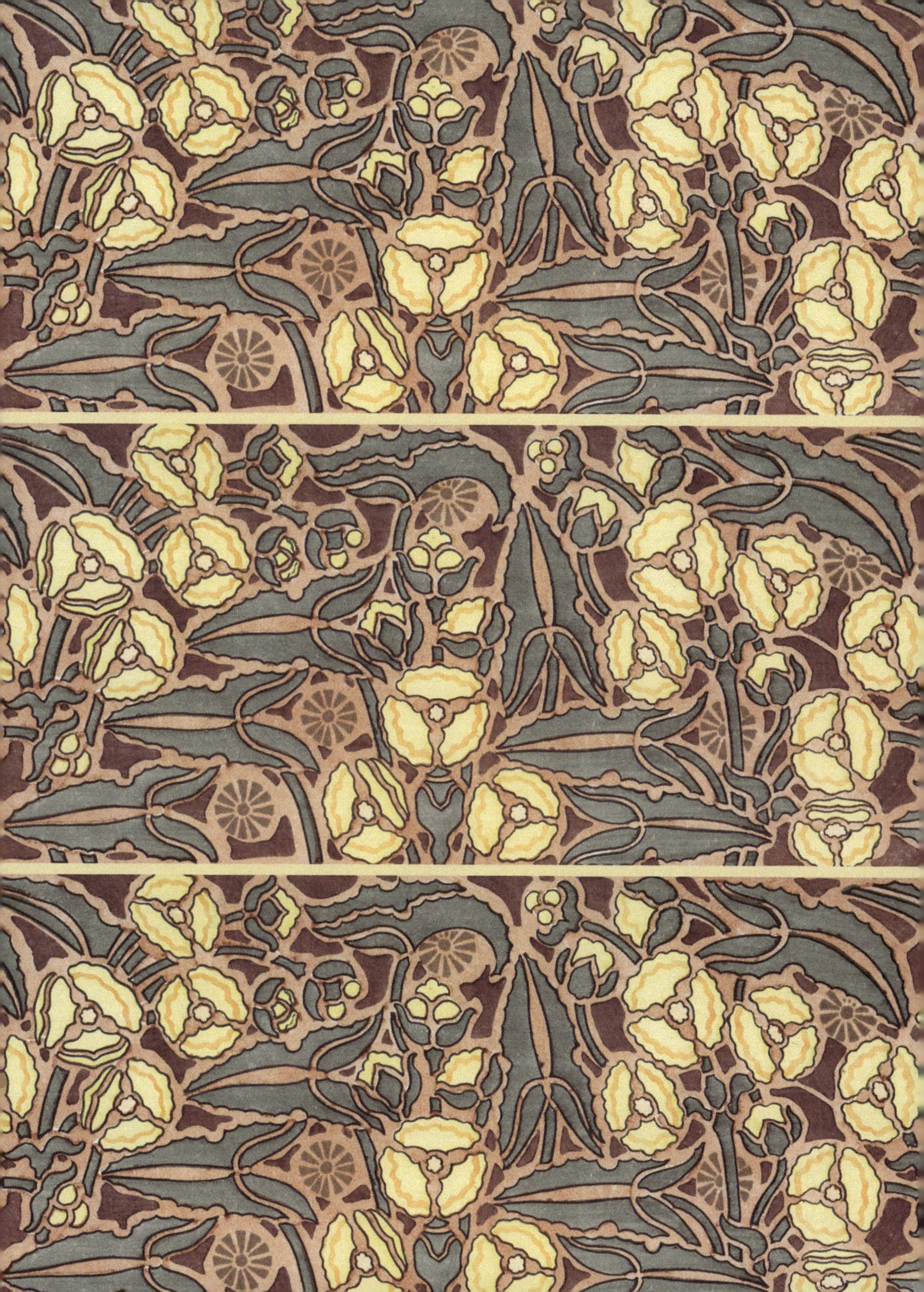

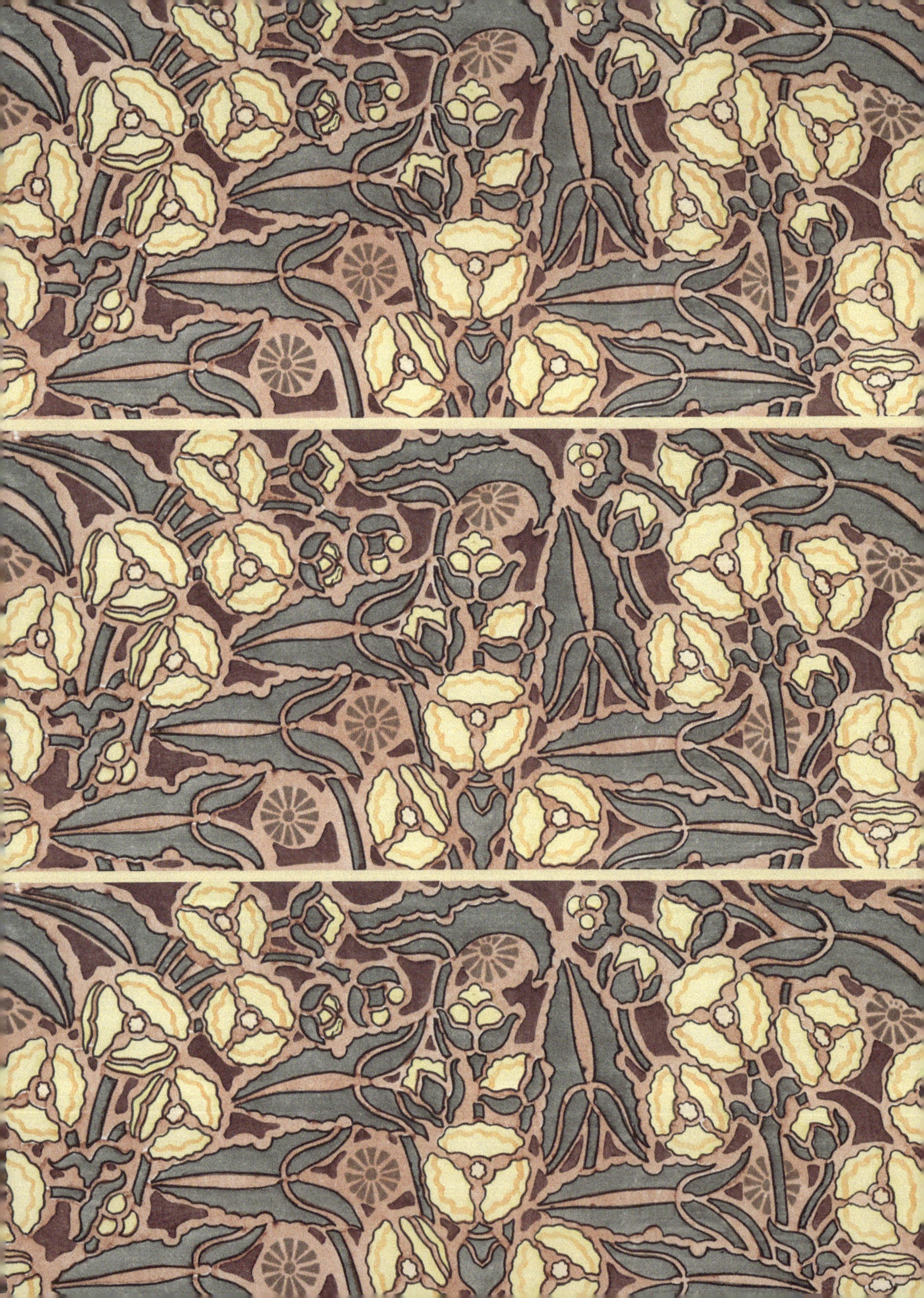

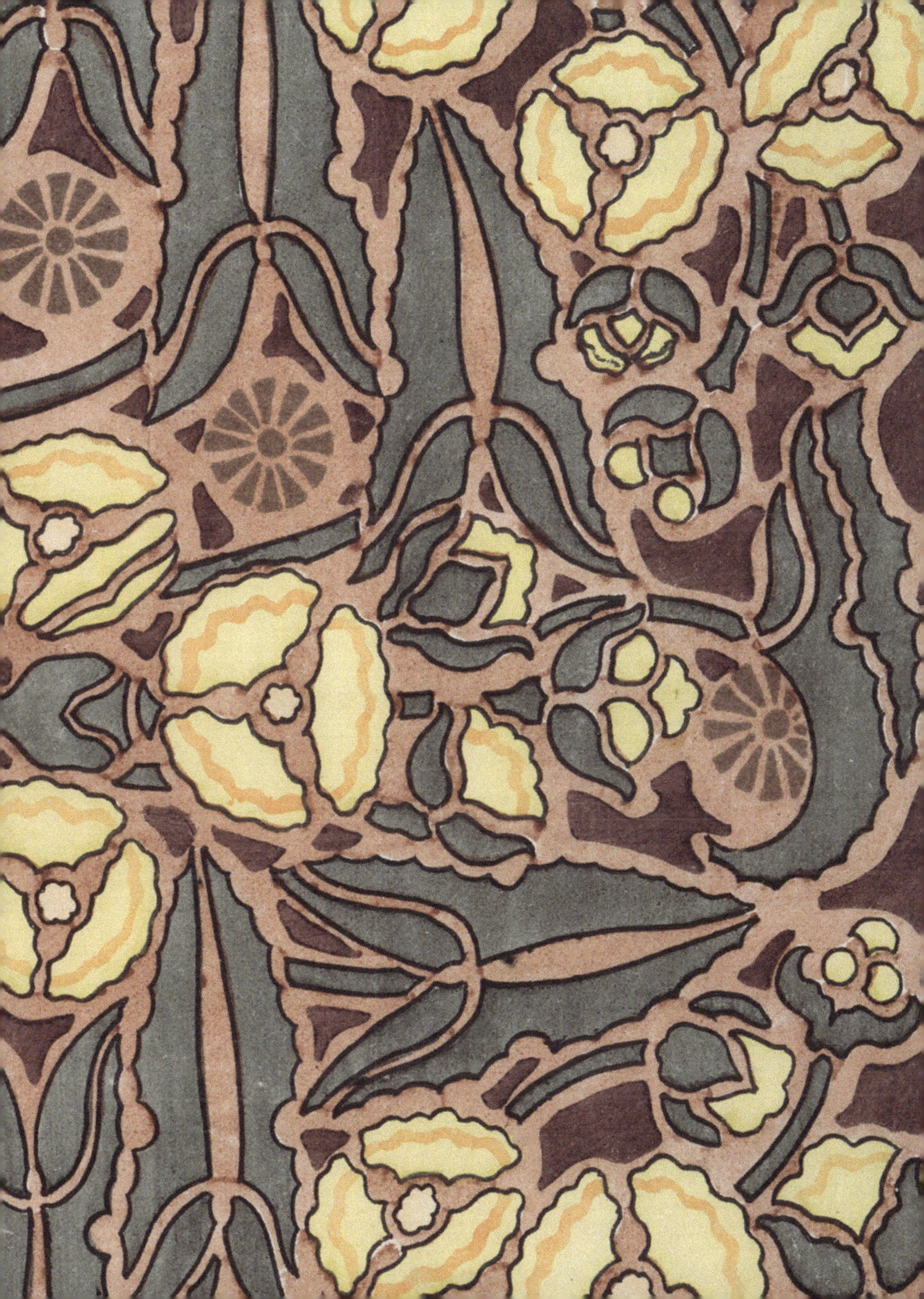

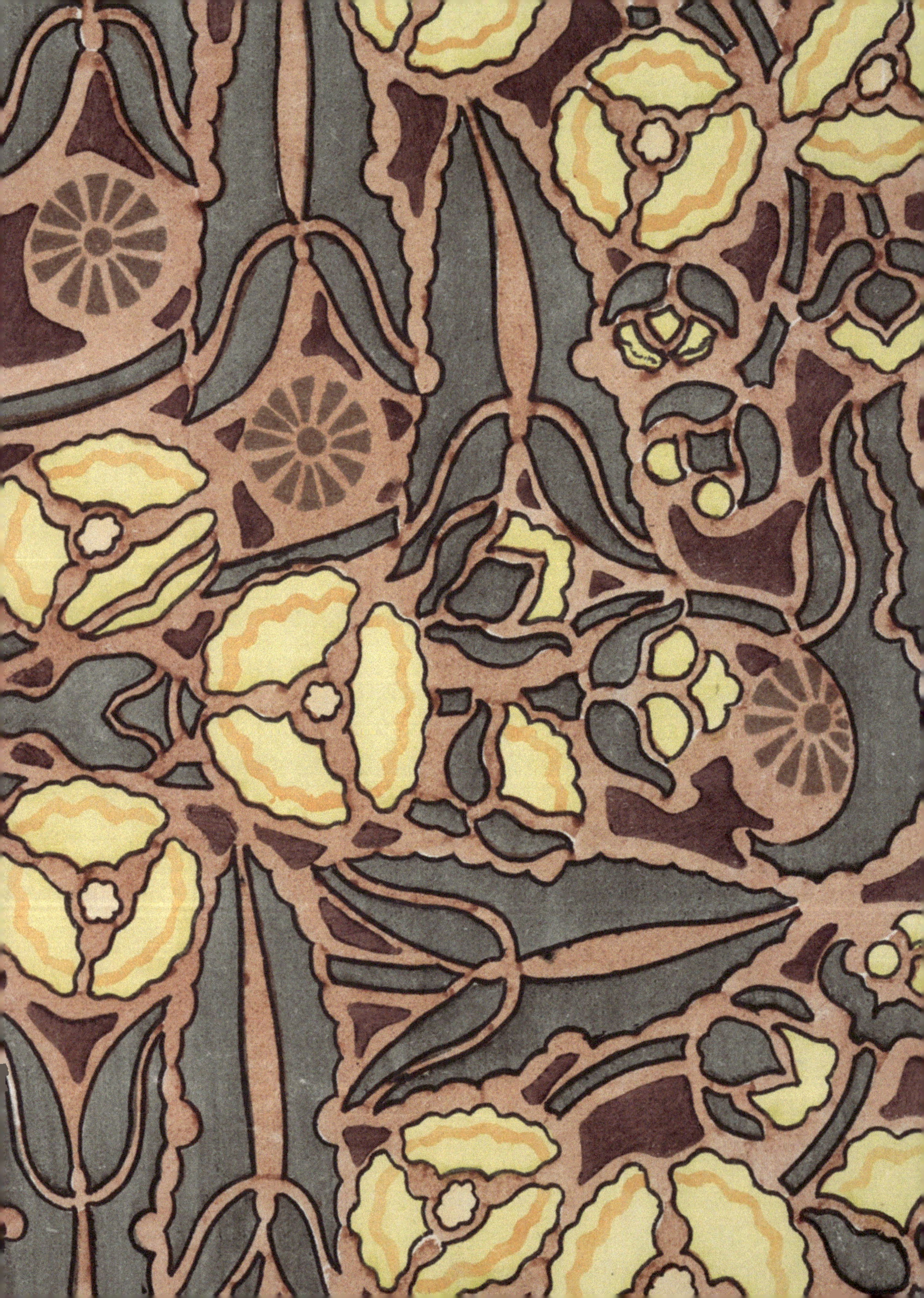

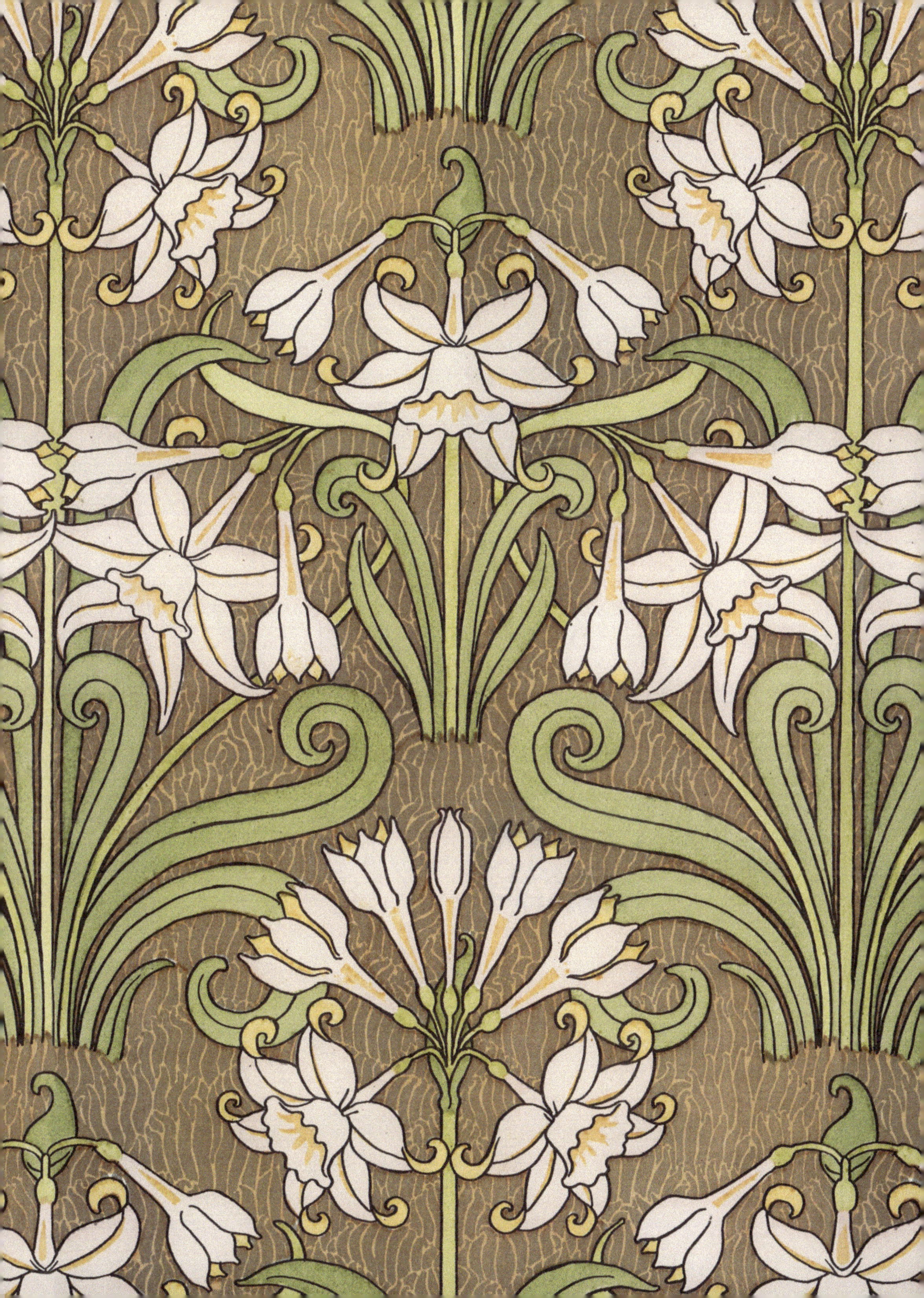

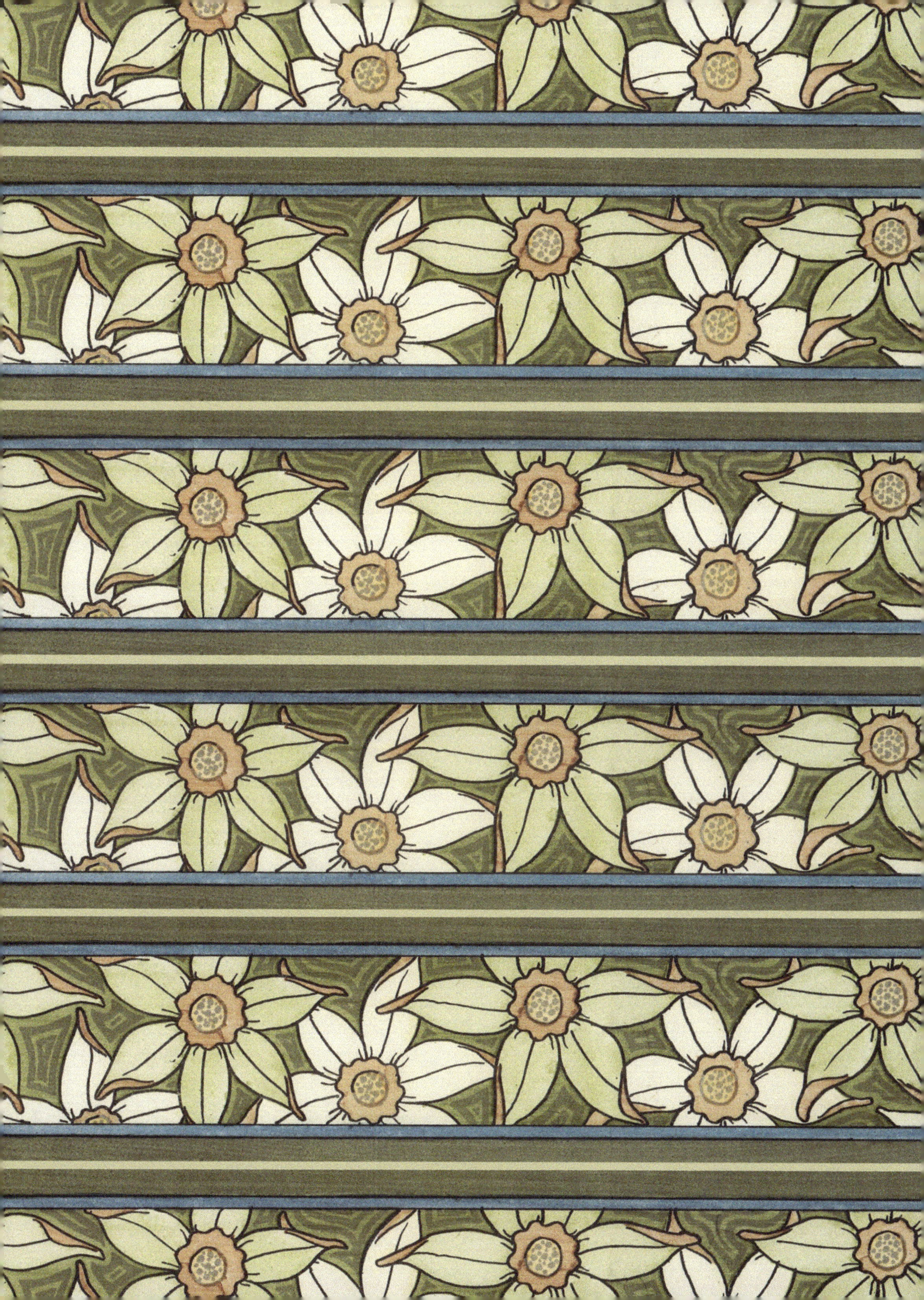

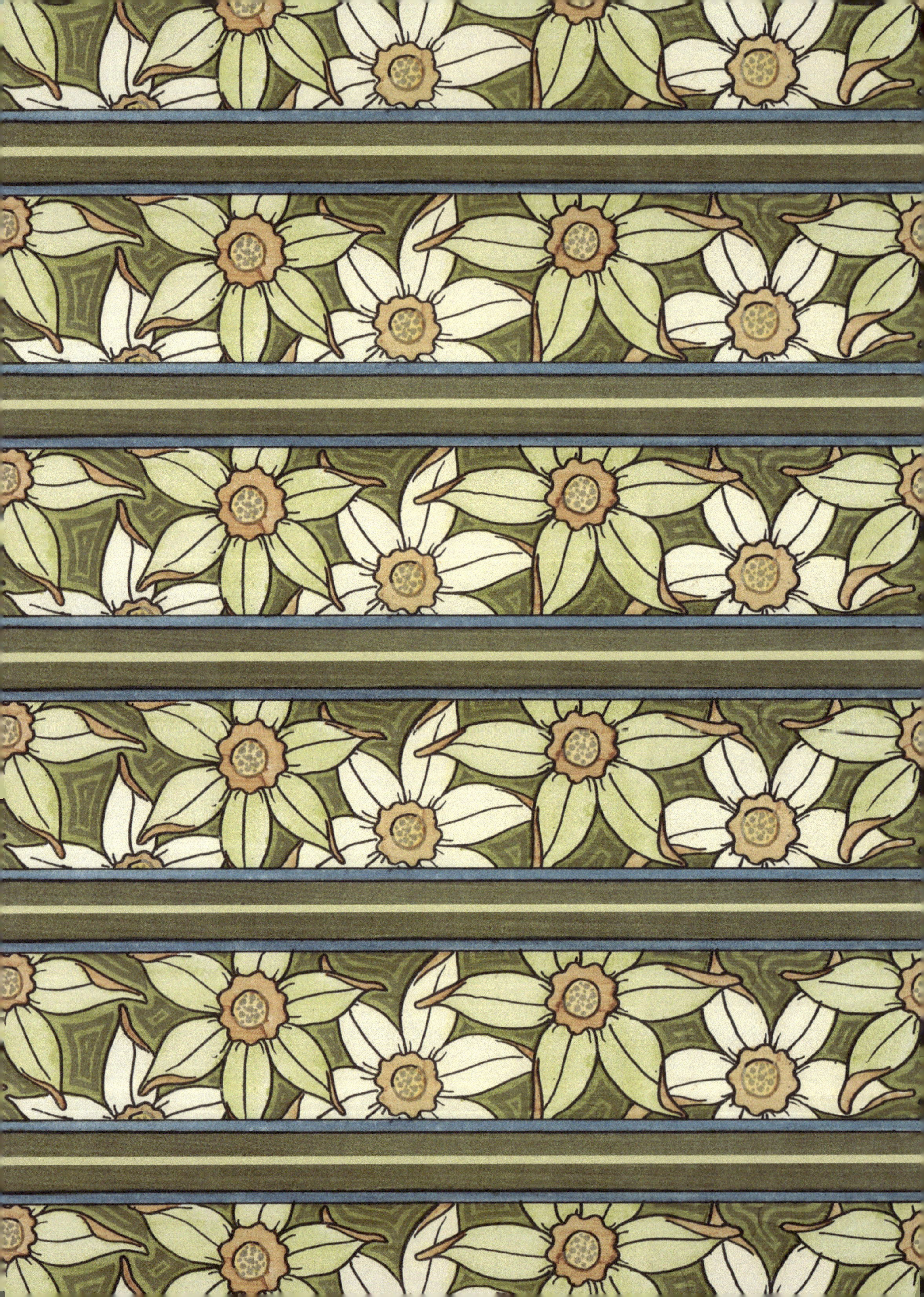

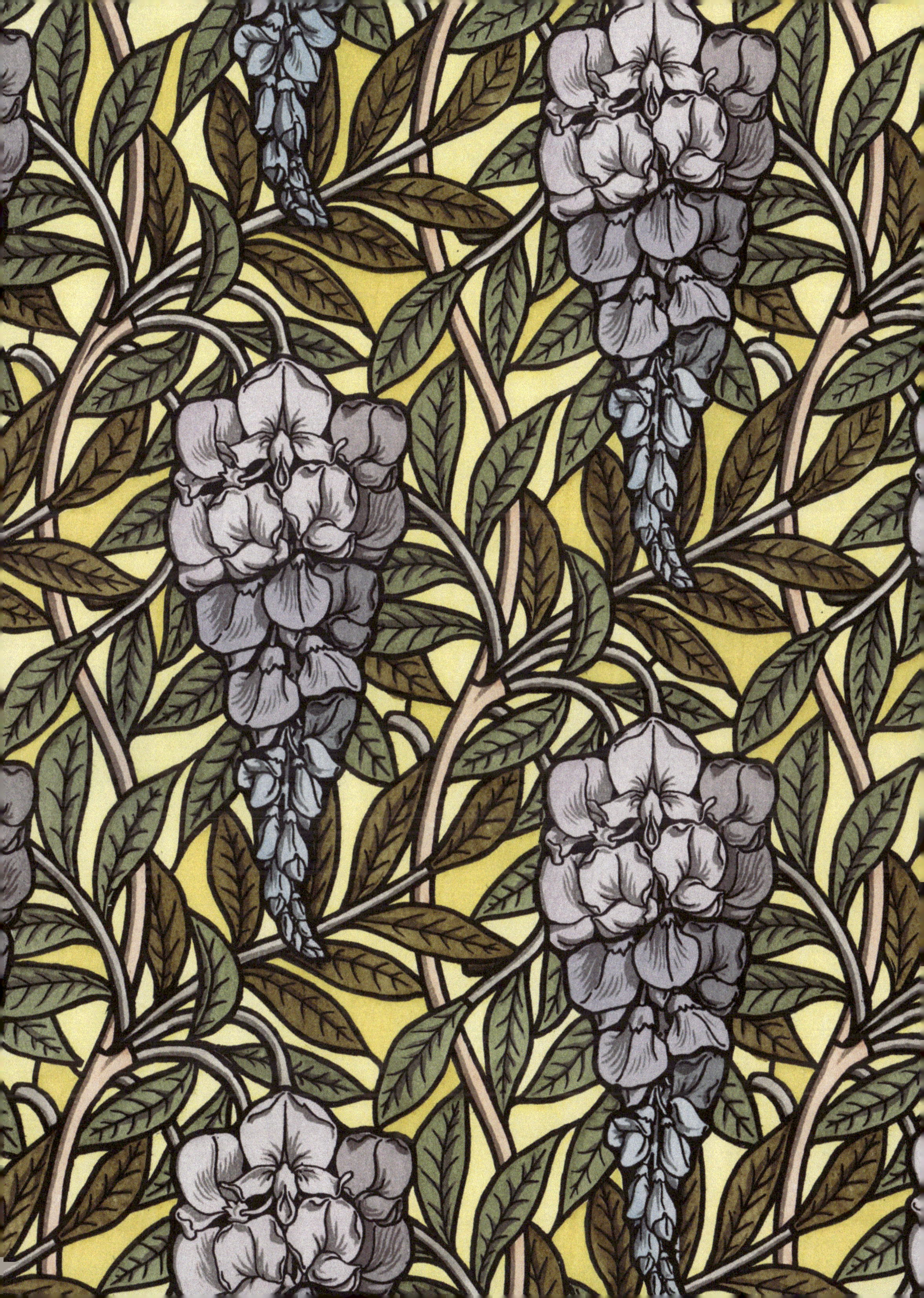

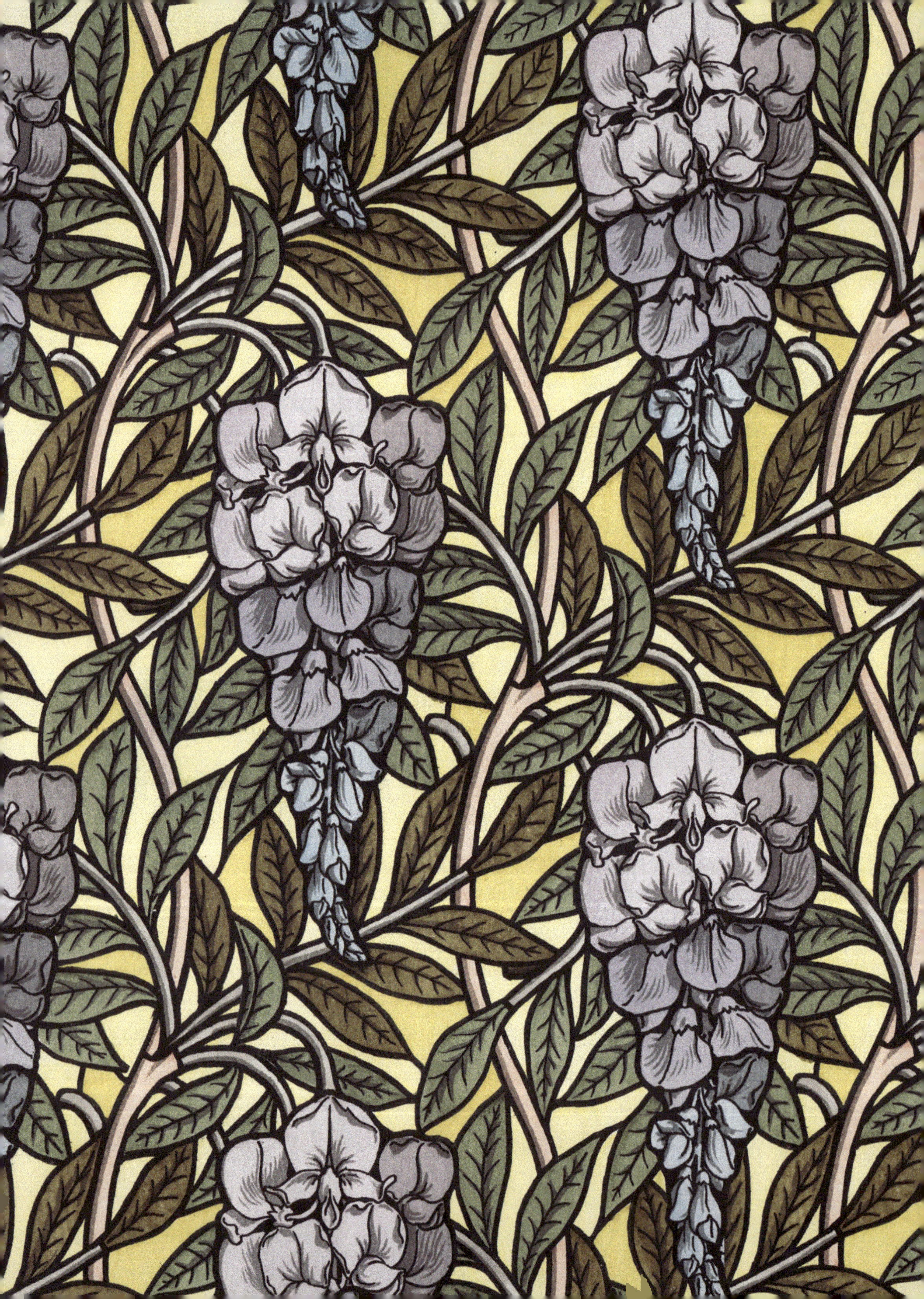